CW00517051

Jewish Lives Project.
Thought

First published in the United Kingdom
by the Jewish Museum London, 2018

British Library cataloguing-in-Publication Data
A catalogue record for this book is available from
the British Library

ISBN 978-1-9998246-3-1

Jewish Museum London
Raymond Burton House
Albert Street, Camden Town
London NW1 7NB
Telephone: 020 7284 7384

Jacket: the illustration of Sigmund Freud was created
especially for this book series by Laurie Rosenwald.

Cover: the cover pattern is reproduced from selected
biography images from within the book.

Published by the Jewish Museum, London, England
Designed by Webb & Webb Design Limited, London, England
Printed and bound in the U.K.

Opposite Wojciech Stattler, *Maccabees*, 1830-1842. Stattler's painting depicts
Antiochus, the Greek King, demanding submission and subservience from the Jews
which led to the Maccabean revolt lasting from 167 to 160 BC. Their namesake, the
Order of Ancient Maccabeans, was established in 1894 by Herbert Bentwich, to
assist in the work of resettling the Jews in Palestine.

Acknowledgements

This book would not have been possible without the generosity and financial support of the Kirsh Charitable Foundation, and the creative vision of Lord Young. The Jewish Museum London would also like to thank the following individuals who have significantly contributed to the content of Jewish Lives Project. Thought: Jonathan Bennett, Sacha Bennett, David Bownes, Janette Dalley, Katy Ferguson, Langley Fisher, Marina Fiorato, Joe Kerr, Jacqui Lewis, Ian Lillicrapp, Anna Lloyd, Rosalyn Livshin, Abigail Morris, Kathrin Pieren, Joanne Rosenthal, David Rosenberg, Laurie Rosenwald, William Rubinstein, Elizabeth Selby, Sara Semic, Derek Taylor, Brian and James Webb.

Contents

Visit the museum:
Jewish Museum London
Raymond Burton House
Albert Street, Camden Town
London NW1 7NB

Preface

Abigail Morris
Director, Jewish Museum London

There is a common adage that says: two Jews, three opinions. This may be best illustrated by a joke. After all, what Jewish truths are not best encountered through humour? The joke goes like this:

A man is rescued from a desert island after 20 years. The news media, amazed at this feat of survival, fly reporters to the island. "How did you survive? How did you keep sane?" they ask. "I had my faith. My faith as a Jew kept me strong." He leads them to an opulent synagogue, made entirely from palm fronds, coconut shells and woven grass. The cameramen take pictures of everything — even a Torah made from banana leaves and written in octopus ink. "This took me five years to complete." "Amazing! And what did you do for the next fifteen years?" "Come with me." He leads them to a shady grove, where there is an even more beautiful synagogue. "This one took me twelve years to complete!" "But sir" asks the reporter, "Why did you build two synagogue?"

Well said the man, "This is the synagogue I attend. That other place? Hah! I wouldn't set foot in that other synagogue if you PAID me!"

In this joke the Jew doesn't even agree with himself. Hegel might have called this dialectics but there is no doubt that the Jewish tradition of debate and arguing has contributed to the building of some very fine minds whether it be Marx, Freud or Klein.

There are many Jews who have created new intellectual traditions, particularly in the last two hundred years. Before the enlightenment Jewish studying had to be based on 'Torah and Talmud'. The Torah is generally taken to mean the Bible but interestingly the word also means teaching. Studying the Bible may seem relatively straightforward but Jewish learning is always about criticism, layering and, of course, arguing. It is, in essence, the opposite of fundamentalism. The Talmud is the commentary on the Bible and it is arranged in a unique way. It has the core text in the centre and then columns of text arranged around it in a sort of concentric pattern. These columns contain commentary on the commentary, or rather arguments about arguments. These represent rabbis and rabbinic schools of debate and they are debating everything from how often a woman can demand sex from her husband (if you're interested, it depends on how physical a job he does!) to intricate pieces of legal interpretation of Jewish laws. Great scholars over the centuries have studied this and added their thoughts and the arguments can sound like they're between two rabbis in a room. But actually, they may be between people arguing across the generations.

Interpretation is all. There is not one truth but there are many paths. A single verse or even a word in the Bible can be analysed and fought over resulting in multiple meanings and vast differences of interpreted analysis. Each page of the Talmud contains a multitude of opinions and arguments. To compound

and complicate this multi stranded interpretation. There is, in fact even more than one Talmud! There is one from Babylon and one from Jerusalem.

Studying together means arguing. Jewish study houses are incredibly noisy places where people shout and bang the tables as they debate their various positions. Post emancipation, Jews have had the opportunity to take these skills and transfer them to the wider world. They have used their finely tuned argumentative minds to tackle political, psychological and philosophical issues. Many of them quite vociferously rejected traditional Judaism but still benefitted from the tradition of vigorous questioning.

Thus, there are some exceptional minds represented in this book. Some who have quite literally changed how we view ourselves and the world. If you don't agree, you can comfort yourself that you too are entering in to a very Jewish questioning and argumentative way of thinking!

Previous René Magritte, *Les vacances de Hegel* (Hegel's Holiday), 1958. Magritte described this painting as the "...thought that Hegel ...would have been very sensitive to this object which has two opposing functions: at the same time not to admit any water (repelling it) and to admit it (containing it). He would have been delighted, I think, or amused (as on a vacation) and I call the painting Hegel's Holiday."
Opposite Carl Schleicher, *Eine Streitfrage aus dem Talmud* (A Talmud Dispute), 1860s.

The British Museum Reading Room, Karl Marx famously spent long hours in here working on what would become his most iconic work, *Das Capital*.

Introduction: Jewish Thought in Britain

Professor William D. Rubinstein
Historian and author

As with any other group of people, it is very difficult to generalise about the nature of "Jewish Thought" in Britain, although some interesting patterns may be discerned. While British Jewry has never comprised more than one per cent of the total population, it has often produced a range of cultural contributors who were of great importance in defining the nature of British culture. In recent decades this impact has increased, as barriers to full participation in the British mainstream have fallen away.

Some of the ways in which Jews have contributed to British culture are unexpected and little-known, as the varied biographies in this volume demonstrate. From journalists to economists and philosophers, Jewish writers and thinkers have helped shape what it means to be British. For instance, many of the ways in which British history and culture were depicted and memorialised during the 19th and early 20th centuries were the work of three intellectuals of Jewish descent. The first Deputy Keeper of the Public Record Office in London was Sir Francis Palgrave. He was born Francis Ephraim Cohen, the son of Meyer Cohen, a Jewish stockbroker, and Rachel (née Levie)

Cohen. A solicitor and later a barrister, Francis Cohen changed his
name to Palgrave in 1823 when he married Elizabeth Turner, whose
mother's maiden name it was; he also converted to Anglicanism. From
1838 until his death he headed the newly established Public Record
Office (PRO). The PRO collected and preserved the most significant
British historical records and documents, in the process defining
what was meant by significant primary historical sources. After 1851
anyone could copy out any of the historical documents held at the
PRO, making possible historical research based on primary sources.

Remarkably, Palgrave's son Francis Turner Palgrave compiled
the first and most famous anthology of English poetry, *The Golden
Treasury of English Songs and Lyrics* (1861), which has been reissued
with revisions ever since and was the progenitor of the many
subsequent anthologies of English poetry, such as the *Oxford Book
of English Verse*. Palgrave had to decide which poems to include (and
exclude), in the process passing judgement on what was meritorious
in English poetry down the ages.

The third of the significant Anglo-Jewish arbiters of British history
was Sir Sidney Lee. Born Sidney Lazarus Lee, the son of Lazarus
Lee (né Levy), a London merchant, he was educated at the City of
London School and at Oxford. In 1883 Lee became Assistant Editor
of the *Dictionary of National Biography* (*DNB*), the great multi-volume
biographical dictionary of thousands of notable people throughout
British history. The *DNB*'s first editor was Sir Leslie Stephen and
when Stephen died in 1904, Lee succeeded him, taking the work to
its conclusion in 1900 and beyond. Lee wrote no fewer than 820 of
its entries, with his sister Elizabeth Lee writing over 80 more entries
on famous British women. Lee wrote the longest and, in many ways,
most important entry in the DNB, on William Shakespeare, which
he later expanded into a well-known book on the life of the Bard. It

may seem remarkable that, in Victorian times, the second editor of the authoritative work of national biography should have been an English Jew, but this was the case.

Even more significant were three 19th-century figures resident in Britain who were instrumental in engendering the three ideological positions of conservatism, liberalism and (extreme) socialism – Benjamin Disraeli, David Ricardo and Karl Marx. All were, in a sense, outsiders to the mainstream British "Establishment", although Ricardo served in parliament while Disraeli, of course, became Prime Minister. Benjamin Disraeli began as a radical but became the ideological leader of modern conservatism after the repeal of the Corn Laws in 1846 split the Tory Party. He was also a noted novelist, penning a series of still-read novels from *Vivian Grey* (1826) to *Endymion* (1880), and a great phrasemaker. He coined the phrase "a dark horse", for example, to describe an outsider who wins. Disraeli was the son of Isaac D'Israeli, a noted historian and man of letters. As is well known, Isaac had his children baptised as Anglicans when Benjamin was 12, after an extended quarrel with his synagogue, Bevis Marks. Benjamin Disraeli remained obsessed with his Jewish background, evolving a unique view of Jews as an ancient aristocratic people destined to lead the gentiles. More significantly, he is seen as the originator of "Tory democracy" and of the tradition of "One Nation Toryism" that held sway in the Conservative Party for a century, as well as reigniting support for the maintenance and expansion of the British Empire.

Although not as well-known as Disraeli or Marx, David Ricardo was, next to Adam Smith, the most influential of the "classical economists". Like Disraeli, Ricardo was of Sephardi descent, the son of a successful stockbroker. Like Disraeli, he left Judaism, in his case when he married a Quaker woman and then became a Unitarian. Ricardo invented many of the basic concepts of classical economics, including the accepted definitions of rent, wages and profits; the notion of comparative advantage; the law of diminishing returns; and the labour theory of value. He was an uncompromising free trade liberal who provided much of the intellectual underpinnings of classical liberalism and was an opponent of slavery and of the death penalty for forgery. Ricardo served in parliament, where he was an influential backbencher, from 1818 until his death. He was a wealthy stockbroker and landowner who left a fortune when he died.

Karl Marx was, of course, by far the most important of the trio in terms of his long-term influence, although during his lifetime he was little known in Britain, where he lived from 1849 until his death in 1883, famously writing *Das Kapital* in the British Museum library. With his associate Friedrich Engels – like Marx, German-born and resident in England, but unlike him an "Aryan" Protestant – Marx developed the theory of dialectical materialism, which became the basis of communism, a doctrine that at one time governed one-third of the world's population. Marx was the descendant of a long line of rabbis, although his father converted to Christianity before his son's birth. Marx was, of course, an atheist, whose view of Jews was wholly negative, arguably antisemitic. He had no associations with the Anglo-Jewish community, most of whom were unaware of his existence, and debatably had little influence on the development of the British labour movement or later of the Labour Party, in contrast to socialist parties and movements on the Continent. Marx is, however, still widely regarded as a highly sophisticated historian and sociologist whose impact has been felt among many disciplines and genres, entirely apart from his posthumous, often appalling, political influence.

Despite the importance of these men, Jews actually contributed little of great distinction to British thought or culture until the 20th century. With the possible exception of Disraeli, none of the great novelists, poets or playwrights in Britain down to the mid-20th century were Jews, and only a handful were of the second rank. The Anglo-Jewish community was very small and, although generally well accepted and subject to few antisemitic restrictions, remained largely outside of the public school and Oxbridge Establishment from which so many British leaders in every field were drawn, and were generally engaged in commerce rather than in the professions. London-born Israel Zangwill was a noted writer (and Zionist leader) who coined the phrase "the melting pot" to describe American society and who wrote the first "locked room" detective novel, *The Big Bow Mystery* (1892). Australian-born Samuel Alexander was a major philosopher at Manchester University, whose work *Space, Time, and Deity* (1920) was influential.

Jewish intellectual life in Britain was, however, transformed by the arrival of what the Marxist historian Perry Anderson famously described as the "white emigration" – "white" in contrast to "red", a reference to their politics, not their skin colour. In his view this group included Ludwig Wittgenstein, Bronislaw Malinowski, Sir Lewis Namier, Sir Karl Popper, Sir Ernst Gombrich, Hans Jürgen Eysenck and Melanie Klein, all of whom were migrants to Britain from the Continent and all of whom, with the exception of Malinowski, were of Jewish descent. (Among others, Arthur Koestler, who was Jewish, and Friedrich Hayek, who was an "Aryan", should clearly be added to this list.) What united these very disparate thinkers, apart from their eminence in very different disciplines, was their anti-Marxism and anti-radicalism, implicit if not explicit, and their admiration – again, implicit if not explicit – for British society and the way that it had peacefully evolved over the centuries. Most were specifically opposed to communism, and to any European totalitarian ideology, from which they had often suffered directly. This list – which was never a group of associates, only a listing of thinkers with somewhat similar backgrounds and attitudes – had arguably the most significant impact on 20th-century British culture of any small body of intellectuals. It also arguably transformed the intellectual status of Jews in British society from marginal to central. Some were explicitly Tories, like Sir Lewis Namier (né Bernstein), the great Polish-born historian of the 18th-century British aristocracy, and Sir Karl Popper, whose *The Open Society and Its Enemies* (1945) and other works discredited the claims of Marxism to be "scientific". Others, like Koestler, were of the democratic left or (like Wittgenstein) were non-political. In Britain, they found intellectual allies with similar views, for instance George Orwell, whose two great novels of the 1940s discredited Stalinism.

It was of course the case that there were very significant Jewish intellectuals clearly on the political left, for example the political theorist Harold Laski and the historians Isaac Deutscher and Eric Hobsbawm. While, until the 1970s, most British Jews voted for the Labour Party, it is probably fair to say that most distinguished Anglo-Jewish intellectuals of the past 80 years have been on the moderate right, while remaining well aware of their Jewish background. Sir Martin Gilbert, Churchill's official biographer and a historian of the Holocaust and of the State of Israel, is a notable example of this. It appears that the current political stance of Anglo-Jewry differs quite considerably from that of the Jewish community in the United States, with its continuing left-liberal preferences, although alongside the largely Jewish neoconservative movement. That the western world's extreme left has, since 1967, largely demonised the State of Israel, often in terms indistinguishable from the far right, has also apparently accentuated the political shift of Anglo-Jewry during the past 50 years.

It is also the case that few notable Jewish intellectual figures have conformed to the antisemitic stereotype of Jews as culture wreckers and destroyers. During the interwar period, the famous sculptor Sir Jacob Epstein, with his (at the time) shockingly non-representative works, was one of the few who could be said to be a destructive cultural modernist. Ironically, however, some important cultural modernists such as T. S. Eliot have been accused of antisemitism.

Since the 1960s there has also been a great broadening of the range of Jewish cultural and intellectual achievement in Britain in many fields, ranging from journalism to medicine to academic life, as the biographies in this book series attest. This is a tribute to the wide acceptance of Jews in recent British society, and the lack of barriers to their ability to achieve, however much antisemitism remains. In many areas, the prominence of British Jews is particularly striking. For example, the list of notable recent British playwrights includes Harold Pinter, who was awarded the Nobel Prize in Literature; Steven Berkoff; Sir Peter Shaffer and his brother Anthony Shaffer; Sir Tom Stoppard and Sir Arnold Wesker, among others. There have been three Jews among recent Lord Chief Justices of England: Sir Peter Taylor, Sir Harry Woolf and Sir Nicholas Phillips.

Another related field in which British Jews have been particularly notable since 1945 is publishing, where such figures as Sir George Weidenfeld, André Deutsch, Frank Cass, Sir Victor Gollancz, Paul Hamlyn, Tom Maschler, Walter Neurath, Dame Gail Rebuck,

Frederick Warburg and others have been among the most visible and innovative of post-war British publishers.

Within the religion of Judaism, there have been only a few British Jews who have been significant internationally, compared with pre-war Europe, the United States and Israel. Among the more prominent Jewish writers on religion since Georgian times have been Rabbi Simeon Singer, translator of the standard prayer book used by the mainstream United Synagogue; Claude Goldsmid Montefiore, a founder of Liberal Judaism in Britain and an important theological writer; Rabbi Louis Jacobs, whose published works led to the "Jacobs Affair" of the 1960s and the foundation of the Masorti movement in Judaism; and two recent chief rabbis, Immanuel Jakobovits, greatly admired by Margaret Thatcher for his conservative views, and Jonathan Sacks, a widely respected and prolific author.

In selecting entries for this fourth volume in the *Jewish Lives* series, the editorial team has concentrated on individuals most associated with their contribution to the development and expression of ideas (however broadly that might be interpreted). Other volumes in the series focus specifically on the Arts, Public Service, Commerce Sport and Science. To avoid too much overlap, some significant thinkers appear elsewhere in the series where they are defined primarily by an alternative distinction (for example, artist, politician or scientist).

Finally, the book series only features people who are no longer with us. If you want to find out about thousands of other British Jews past and present and their contributions to British society, visit www.JewishLivesProject.com

Jacob Epstein, *St Michael's Victory over the Devil*, 1958, Coventry Cathedral

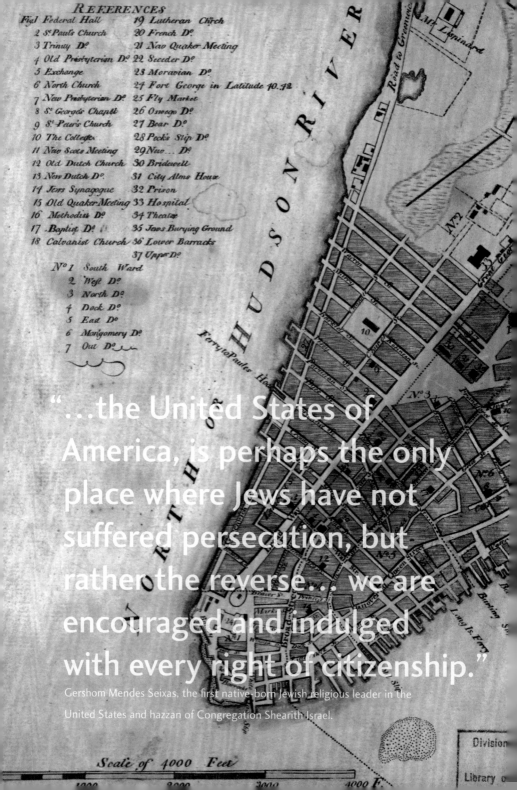

REFERENCES

Fig 1 Federal Hall
2 St Pauls Church
3 Trinity Do.
4 Old Presbyterian Do.
5 Exchange
6 North Church
7 New Presbyterian Do.
8 St George's Chapel
9 St Peter's Church
10 The College
11 New Scots Meeting
12 Old Dutch Church
13 New Dutch Do.
14 Jews Synagogue
15 Old Quaker Meeting
16 Methodist Do.
17 Baptist Do.
18 Calvanist Church

19 Lutheran Chirch
20 French Do.
21 New Quaker Meeting
22 Seceder Do.
23 Moravian Do.
24 Fort George in Latitude 40.42
25 Fly Market
26 Oswego Do.
27 Bear Do.
28 Peck's Slip Do.
29 New... Do.
30 Bridewell
31 City Alms House
32 Prison
33 Hospital
34 Theatre
35 Jews Burying Ground
36 Lower Barracks
37 Upper Do.

No 1 South Ward
2 West Do.
3 North Do.
4 Dock Do.
5 East Do.
6 Montgomery Do.
7 Out Do.

"…the United States of America, is perhaps the only place where Jews have not suffered persecution, but rather the reverse… we are encouraged and indulged with every right of citizenship."

Gershom Mendes Seixas, the first native-born Jewish religious leader in the United States and hazzan of Congregation Shearith Israel.

Scale of 4000 Feet

1000   2000   3000   4000 F.

Division

Library of

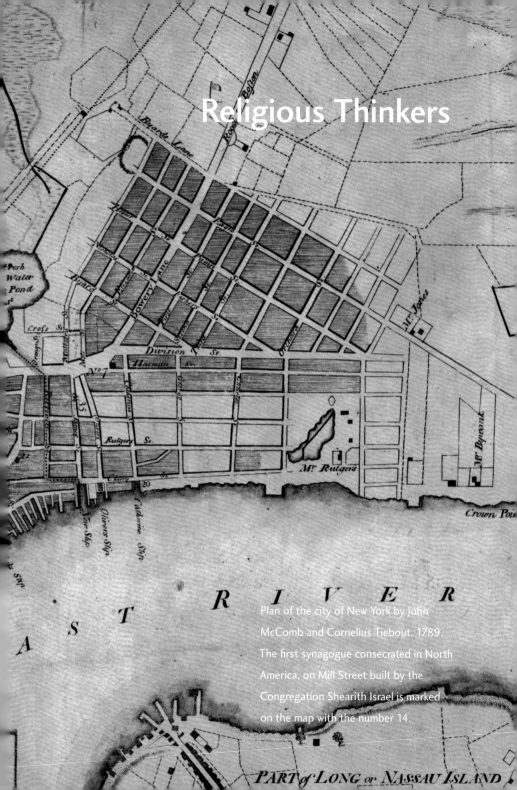

Religious Thinkers

Plan of the city of New York by John McComb and Cornelius Tiebout, 1789. The first synagogue consecrated in North America, on Mill Street built by the Congregation Shearith Israel is marked on the map with the number 14.

The Great Synagogue, London. In this photograph by Cecil Beaton, Reverend Hermann Mayerowitsch surveys the rubble and debris of the Great Synagogue, following a devastating air raid on the evening of Saturday 10 May 1941.

Religious Thinkers

Derek Taylor
Author and former editor
of the 'Jewish Year Book'

Jewish religious thinkers fall into two categories: those who interpret the traditional written and oral bodies of law, and those who decide that they need changing, updating or even abolishing. For the Orthodox, the written and oral laws are sacrosanct. For the others, they are not.

In Britain, the Jews were officially readmitted by Charles II in 1661. They were mostly Sephardim from Holland, where they had fled over the years from Spain, after the Jews were expelled in 1492. Most knew little of the faith, as it had been passed down in secret from parents to children, with the threat of execution hanging over them if they were found out. The first official spiritual leader of the Sephardim in London was Haham Jacob Sasportas (1664–5). The kinds of problem he had to deal with were, for example, could a man be a member of the community if he hadn't been circumcised? Sasportas said "no". It was that fundamental.

The Sephardim settled down and the Ashkenazim started to arrive from Germany and eastern Europe. They were poor refugees from oppression and discrimination in their own countries and were treated by the Sephardim as second-class citizens. Even so, they were far more knowledgeable and religious than most of the Sephardim and had tutors like Joseph ben Menachem Menke from Leipnik, Simcha Binem from Pintschau, Moses ben Judah from Posen and Judah ben Mordechai Cohen from Amsterdam.

It became a necessary custom to import rabbis from the Continent. Of the over 20 Chief Rabbis and Hahamim since 1664, only three were born in Britain. The British Jewish community did not grow its own Talmudic experts for hundreds of years. There could have been a Yeshivah (a seminary for studying the Talmud) when Elias de Pass left a legacy to create one in 1743, but the Lord Chancellor ruled that it couldn't be used for that purpose as it was going to be "in contradiction of the Christian religion." Chief Rabbi Hart Lyon (1756–1763) tried to start one as well but there were few recruits. So he resigned and went back to Germany, where he had been promised students.

The Ashkenazim built the Great Synagogue in the City as the Sephardim had built Bevis Marks. The Great Synagogue would be destroyed in the Blitz in 1940. The two communities had minor differences, due to living geographically far apart over the centuries, but nothing serious. In 1760 they joined together to create the Board of Deputies of British Jews, which still represents British Jews with the authorities today.

The Chief Rabbi of the Ashkenazim and the Haham of the Sephardim were attached to single synagogues but gave advice to whoever had problems relating to Jewish law in other congregations. In 1715, for example, Haham David Nietto (1702–1728) told the lay leaders of Bevis Marks to support the government's choice of George I to succeed Queen Anne. After the American Declaration of Independence (1776), the Sephardi synagogue in New York still looked to the Haham in London for religious decisions.

Where the Ashkenazim formed communities in other British towns, the Sephardim remained at Bevis Marks. This unity continued until 1840 when a number of senior members broke away to form another congregation, which was the origin of the Reform movement. For nearly a century it had very little to do with matters of doctrine.

The Secessionists, as they were called for many years, had moved home from the City to the West End and wanted to create a congregation there. The lay leaders of Bevis Marks didn't want competition and threw them out of the community. The doctrinal exception was David Woolf Marks, the minister of the new congregation, who wanted changes in line with the first Reform congregation in Hamburg in 1819, but he was kept in check by his lay leaders.

Into this communal row came a new Chief Rabbi, Nathan Marcus Adler, from Hanover. He found a community where there were very few sermons from the pulpit, no theological college, no rabbinical families like his own, little care for poor Jews, rivalry between synagogues and no common prayer book. In the next 45 years of his ministry, Adler created the United Synagogue, Jews' College, the Singer prayer book and the origins of Jewish Care and established the British pulpit.

Adler knew his priorities almost from his arrival and he had a unique way of achieving his objectives. When there was opposition, he always pleaded for "peace for my sake". When he achieved his ends, the opposition could say they had given in for the sake of peace and Adler always gave them the credit. Adler was fortunate in that the country's Jewish lay leader was Sir Moses Montefiore, who was Adler's patron and consistent supporter throughout his ministry. Unusually, the lay and religious leaders worked in perfect harmony.

The Secessionists did not flourish in Adler's time, although a new community was created in Manchester, largely because the founders wanted independence from Adler in London. Their new minister was Solomon Marcus Schiller-Szenessy, an immigrant rabbi with credentials as good as Adler's. For a time there was the possibility of competition, but Schiller-Szenessy fell out with his congregation and went off to Cambridge to catalogue the Hebrew manuscripts there.

The Assasination of Tsar Alexander II, Gustav Broling, 1881

Gateshead Yeshiva, some of the first students and staff from the early 1930s.

The Secessionists did build a fine new synagogue in the West End, but the prayers were still in Hebrew and the men and women still sat apart. There was no new Reform synagogue between 1873 and 1919.

In 1870 Adler achieved another of his objectives when the main London congregations joined together as the United Synagogue. Just before he died, he also supervised the creation of a common prayer book to be used in all his synagogues. As he realised he was yesterday's man, though revered, the prayer book was credited to a fashionable young rabbi, Simeon Singer, and has always been known as the Singer prayer book. In the foreword to the first edition, Singer gives the credit to Adler.

After the assassination of Tsar Alexander II in 1881, anti-Jewish pogroms broke out in many parts of eastern Europe and a flood of refugees fled to America, England and South Africa. In 1891 a new community was founded in north London that, eventually, became the Union of Orthodox Hebrew Congregations. Their congregation in Gateshead created the Gateshead Yeshiva, which became the foremost Orthodox powerhouse in the country. Its academic prowess was strengthened in the 1930s by the arrival of a number of eminent Talmudists, who were refugees from the Nazis; men like Leib Lopian, Leib Gurwitz and Naftali Shakowitzky.

Towards the end of the 19th century several leading Jews thought that the Secessionists were not modernising the religion as drastically as they should. Led by Claude Montefiore, they founded the Liberal Synagogue. Montefiore also believed that there was common ground between Christianity and Judaism that should lead to a reconciliation of views. The main selling points of Liberal Judaism were fewer rules, a greater role for women and easier arrangements for conversion. It was financially sound, built a splendid Liberal synagogue opposite Lords cricket ground and possessed in Montefiore a charismatic and powerful leader. To Montefiore's great disappointment, it still didn't catch on to any extent.

At the same time a new movement was developing within Judaism: Zionism. The idea of a national home for the Jews in Palestine created, however, a great deal of opposition. It had the support of the Haham, Moses Gaster, but was opposed by almost all the other communal leaders. Hermann Adler, the Ashkenazi Chief Rabbi after his father, summed up the first Zionist conference as an "egregious blunder", an outstandingly bad and shocking mistake. The trouble was that the community had been trying to confirm its loyalty to the Crown for centuries and saw Zionism as offering antisemites the ammunition to question their true feelings; the potential problem of dual loyalties. To make matters worse, the British Foreign Office saw the Zionist leaders, headquartered in Berlin, as a possible fifth column.

In 1913, however, Joseph Herman Hertz succeeded Hermann Adler. Hertz was a Zionist from South Africa and had loyally supported the British during the Boer War. He was *persona grata* in Whitehall. In 1916 the government floated the idea of the National Home in the hope of bringing the Americans into the war on the Allied side. The president of the Board of Deputies and of the Anglo-Jewish Association wrote to *The Times* to say the British Jews didn't want it. Hertz and Lord Rothschild wrote to say they did. The Balfour Declaration was the result.

Between the wars, Hertz was often at loggerheads with the head of the United Synagogue, who wanted a rapprochement with the Reform movement. They, for their part, wanted it as well, but despaired of it ever happening. In 1929 an American Rabbi, Harold Reinhart, was appointed and persuaded a small representative gathering of his members to join, with the liberals, the World Union of Progressive Judaism. There was now no chance of a reconciliation.

The community did work together in secular areas, particularly in dealing with the problem of refugees from Nazi Germany. In Germany itself, one Rabbi, Leo Baeck (1873–1956), tried to ameliorate the suffering of the Jews but was sent to a concentration camp in 1943 and only narrowly survived. He came to Britain after the war and served as president of the WUPJ. Another Holocaust survivor was Rabbi Hugo Gryn (1930–1996), who came to Britain in 1964 and served as the minister at the main Reform synagogue. Gryn was a prolific broadcaster and a highly respected rabbi.

Hertz was succeeded by Israel Brodie, who had been a chaplain to the forces in both world wars. While Palestine was in the grip of civil war, with the British trying to keep the peace, Brodie's well-proven patriotism was a good advertisement for the community. It was Brodie who later had to deal with the "Jacobs Affair". A brilliant Orthodox rabbi, Louis Jacobs, wrote a book querying some aspects of the Bible. As a result, his career in the Orthodox ranks was stunted, though his former congregants started a new synagogue for him. In future years he would agree to the congregation becoming part of the Masorti movement, which was headquartered in America and not entirely in line with Orthodox practice.

It was during Brodie's time that Jews' College, the seminary founded by Nathan Marcus Adler, reached its apogee with the appointment of Rabbi Kopul Kahana to prepare students for the rabbinical diploma. Many of today's rabbis were taught by Kahana, an expert on Jewish, Roman and English law. Kahana was once asked who was the greatest religious authority in Britain. He replied "Dayan Abramsky, Rabbi Rabinow and myself – but not necessarily in that order!" Kahana taught half the rabbis granted their semicha at Jews' College in its 150 years of existence.

The position of the Reform synagogue at the end of the 20th century was explained by one of its female rabbis, who suggested that we were "in a modern post-enlightenment world, where individual autonomy has taken the place of divine sanction." The Orthodox position was that nothing could take the place of divine sanction and 70 per cent of the British community remained in the Orthodox camp.

When Brodie retired, he was succeeded by Immanuel Jakobovits, an expert on Jewish medical ethics and a former Chief Rabbi of Ireland. There came a time during Margaret Thatcher's time as prime minister, when the Church of England produced a document complaining that the government wasn't doing enough for the poor. Jakobovits was asked to sign it, along with the other clerics, but pointed out that he couldn't, as the Jewish view was that the poor should be helped to stop being poor. This was very much in line with Thatcher's thinking and Jakobovits found himself in the House of Lords. Fifteen years later, one of the first women rabbis, the liberal Julia Neuberger, was also elevated to the Lords.

After Jakobovits came Jonathan Sacks (1991), the most brilliant speaker the community had ever produced. He became what could best be described as the moral voice of the nation. To such an extent that when *The Times* was trying to sum up the causes and results of the 2011 urban riots, it asked Sacks, rather than a Church of England archbishop, to write the article. Sacks also became a peer. When he retired in 2013, the South African Ephraim Mirvis was appointed to succeed him.

The community today numbers about 250,000 and has happily married British values with the Jewish law laid down in the sixth-century Babylonian Talmud.

Opposite Lord's Chamber, Houses of Parliament, London, only Church of England bishops sit in the House by right, however both former Chief Rabbis Immanual Jakobovits and Jonathan Sacks, as well as Rabbi Julia Neuberger have been elevated to the Lords.

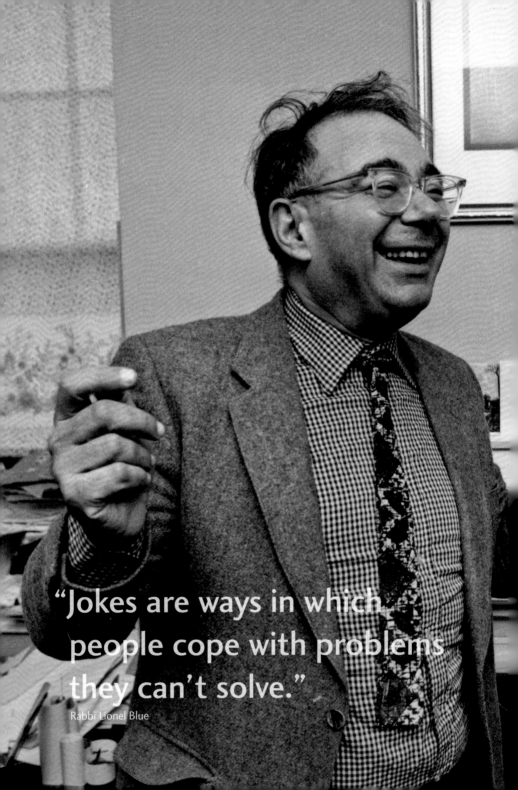

"Jokes are ways in which people cope with problems they can't solve."

Rabbi Lionel Blue

Biographies A – C

Rabbi Lionel Blue, seen here with fellow radio presenter the Reverend Roger Royle, possesed the special ability that breaks through the surface of religious dogma with a well placed joke.

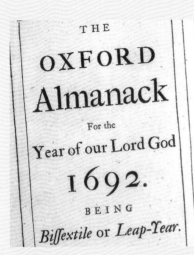

THE

OXFORD

Almanack

For the

Year of our Lord God

1692.

BEING

Biſſextile or *Leap-Year.*

Isaac Abendana

An early scholar of the
Hebrew language
c.1650–c.1710

Isaac Abendana was a mid-17th century Hebrew scholar. His exact birth and death dates are not known. Born in Spain to an observant family, Isaac was the younger brother of Jacob Abendana, the religious head of the Sephardi community. At a time when Protestant England had become interested in the supremacy of biblical writings, Isaac was invited to come to Oxford in order to work on a Latin translation of the *Mishnah* (the Hebrew commentary on Talmudic law). Isaac moved to Trinity College, Cambridge in 1663, only a few years after the readmission of Jews to England in 1656. There he sold his Hebrew books and gave classes on the Hebrew language to all who wished to attend. Returning to Oxford in 1689, Abendana created the *Oxford Almanac*, containing important information about university life as well as introductory essays for non-Jewish students on Jewish law and religion. Isaac was proud of his religion and dedicated much of his life to educating non-Jews about his heritage. Isaac Abendana died suddenly one morning while visiting a colleague; apparently, he "lit his pipe and fell down dead."

Roy Clive Abraham
He codified several
African languages
1890–1963

Roy Clive Abraham was born in
Melbourne, Australia. He studied
at Balliol College, Oxford and
graduated with a first-class
honours degree in oriental
languages. He also studied
anthropology at University College London and classical Arabic at
the School of Oriental Studies, University of London. During the
First World War Abraham served as an officer in Arabia and India, an
opportunity he used to widen his linguistic knowledge by learning
Hindustani. He arrived in Nigeria in 1925 as part of the colonial
administration, eventually becoming an anthropological officer.
While there he began studying African languages, starting with the
Afro-Asian language Bolanci, then collaborating with G.P. Bargery
on the *Hausa-English Dictionary*. Abraham refined Bargery's six-tone
system in his own *Principles of Hausa* (1934), correcting it to a three-
tone system. He later taught the language to troops in the Royal
West African Frontier Force. He returned to England in the 1940s to
teach and became a lecturer in Amharic, the language of Ethiopia,
at the School of Oriental and African Studies at the University of
London. The University of Oxford awarded him the degree of DLitt in
1949 for his works on the Tiv language. Abraham spent his last years
in the field researching native languages, publishing a *Dictionary of
Modern Yoruba* in 1958.

vigorous pen. What his loss signified to the College — ... community may be partially gathered from these words i which the *Jewish Chronicle* lamented his death: —

Alas! alas that we should have to announce such evil tidings! Alas th we should have to record a loss sustained by the community, which ' unhesitatingly designate as calamitous, and which, in some respects, is ir parable! The **Rev. Barnett Abrahams**, B. A., *Dayan* of the Spanish a Portuguese Congregation, and Principal of the Jews' College, expired Sunday morning last, before he had completed the thirty-second year of life!... Virtues which, when possessed by other persons, shine forth v such great lustre, were in him scarcely noticed, because paled by the sid others of still greater brilliancy. His conscientiousness in the disch of his multifarious duties as *Dayan* and teacher, and his labours of love, ' such that from the morning dawn to the midnight hour hardly a mo was allowed for relaxation. He performed all his duties with an e ordinary earnestness, springing from the conviction of the presence of which he always carried in his pure heart. ... There was in the dec an unselfishness and a child-like simplicity, that could not but him the respect of everyone that came into contact with him. He e in and for others; and if he cared for himself it was simply as the wor does for his tool, because this self was necessary for the service of c His love for his God and people, and his zeal for its service wa bounded. In his heart burnt a flame of enthusiasm, which, like the ! the altar of the Lord, brightened and warmed everything around his its genial rays. But the love for his people was not impulsive, not w by fits and starts; it was a passion, it is true, yet under the control strong intellect, and chastened by an observant mind and the hand of ence. He recognized early in life that all communal efforts and all ... Jewish progress, must remain compa

Barnett Abrahams

Principal of Jews' College
1831–1863

Barnett Abrahams was born in Warsaw. He was the son of Abraham Susman and his second wife Esther Reisel. Abraham settled in England in 1839 and Esther and Barnett joined him there in 1841. Abrahams received rabbinical instruction from Chief Rabbi Nathan Marcus Adler, and in 1849 was enrolled in the Spanish and Portuguese congregation's theological college. The elders of the congregation bore the cost of Abrahams' education, first at the City of London School and then at University College London. In 1851 Abrahams was invited to preach at the Bevis Marks synagogue, where he made a favourable impression. In 1854 he was elected assistant dayan (religious judge) at the synagogue, and in 1856 was elected chief of the ecclesiastical court. In 1858 he was elected principal of Jews' College London, the Jewish theological seminary. Abrahams was dedicated to the education of the young, and was a kind and patient teacher. However, in an article published after Abrahams' death, his granddaughter revealed that he had a violent temper, and that his wife kept a supply of crockery for him to smash in order to relieve his feelings.

Israel Abrahams

Scholar and historian
1858–1925

Israel Abrahams was born in
Finsbury Square, London. His
father, Barnett Abrahams, was the
principal of Jews' College, London,
from 1858 until his death. His
mother was Jane, née Brandon.
Abrahams received his Hebrew
instruction from his father, and was educated at Jews' College from
1872. He went on to read philosophy at University College London,
where he graduated MA in 1881. From 1881 to 1903 he lectured in
English and mathematics at Jews' College, where he also founded its
literary society. In 1902 Abrahams became Reader in Talmudic and
Rabbinic Literature at the University of Cambridge. In 1906 he was
made Curator of Oriental Literature in the university library, and in
1907 was elected President of the University of Glasgow's theological
society. From 1889–1908 Abrahams co-edited the *Jewish Quarterly
Review* with Claude Montefiore, and contributed many significant
articles to his own and other periodicals. In 1896 he published his
major work, *Jewish Life in the Middle Ages*. Abrahams was actively involved
in many Jewish societies. He was a founder member of the Society of
Maccabees, and in 1893 of the Jewish Historical Society in England. He
was sympathetic to the views of Lily Montagu in the founding of Liberal
Judaism and conducted the first service at the Liberal Jewish Synagogue
in 1911. The library of the synagogue was subsequently named after
him. In 1925, the year of his death, he received a presentation from the
University of Cambridge in recognition of his services to the students.

Chimen Abramsky
He pioneered the field
of Jewish studies
1916–2010

Chimen Abramsky was born into
an Orthodox family in modern-
day Belarus. After being accused
of treason, Abramsky's father
Yehezkel found refuge in Britain
in 1932, where he became one
of the most senior rabbis in the country. Abramsky soon became
involved in the lively Jewish community of London's East End and
found work in Shapiro, Valentine & Co., the oldest Jewish bookstore
in the area. On the publication of his book, *Karl Marx and the British
Labour Movement*, he was invited, with the help of Isaiah Berlin, to a
position at Oxford University. From there, he moved to University
College London, becoming head of the department of Hebrew and
Jewish Studies in 1974. Abramsky is regarded as a pioneer in the field
of Jewish studies, helping to establish it as an emerging academic
discipline. Abramsky was famous for his vast personal library, which
included Karl Marx's personally annotated copy of *The Communist
Manifesto*. At 5ft tall, Abramsky would often have to ask visitors
to reach volumes for him. While Abramsky was not observant, and
would dive onto the floor of the car when being driven through the
more religious areas of London, he was nevertheless proud of his
Jewish heritage.

Yehezkel Abramsky

Rabbinic scholar and
Orthodox Jewish leader
1886–1976

Yehezkel Abramsky was born
in Dashkovtsy, Lithuania. His
parents were Mordecai Zalman
Abramsky, a timber merchant,
and Freydel Goldin. A promising
Talmudic student, he trained
at a series of yeshivoth (seminaries) and earned his certification as
a rabbi before he was 18. He became so well thought of in Russia
as a jurisconsult that he was refused permission to leave. Abramsky
became embroiled in the debate about religious freedom and spent
months eluding arrest. In 1929 he was arrested and sentenced to
five years' hard labour in Siberia. Following diplomatic intervention
Abramsky came to London in 1932 as rabbi of the right-wing
Orthodox community. Anthony Eden, then British foreign secretary,
secured the release of his sons, who joined Abramsky in London
in 1937. Abramsky was naturalised as a British subject in the same
year and was later invited to head the ecclesiastical court of the
United Synagogue. His reputation as a speaker was unrivalled in
the community, and his London discourses (delivered in Yiddish)
drew large audiences. Yet Abramsky's life's work was not spoken but
written. The 24-volume *Hazon Yehezkel*, a commentary on the *Tosefta*,
a digest of Jewish Law dating from c.200 AD, was begun in 1925 and
completed in 1975. Abramsky even continued this work during his
internment in Siberia, smuggling his writings out on cigarette paper.

Hermann Adler
Chief Rabbi
1839–1911

Hermann Adler was born in Hanover. His father was Nathan Marcus Adler, chief rabbi of Hanover, and his mother was Henrietta Worms. In 1845 the family moved to London. Nathan Adler became the chief rabbi of the United Hebrew Congregations. Hermann was educated at University College School, and went on to study at University College London, where he graduated in 1854. In 1860 his father sent him to Prague for rabbinical instruction, and two years later he was ordained. In 1862 he was awarded a PhD from the University of Leipzig for a thesis on druidism. Returning to London, Adler was appointed temporary principal of Jews' College in 1863, and the following year became the first minister at the Bayswater synagogue. Adler was both preacher and teacher; he elevated the sermon to an art form, and committed himself to the provision of Jewish instruction in East End schools. Adler came to be regarded as the acceptable face of Jewish Orthodoxy. He formed close friendships with non-Jews in high places and moved in the loftiest social circles; the future King Edward VII is said to have referred to him as "my chief rabbi". But his relationships with his own community were more problematic. He identified with the anti-Zionist position and was opposed to any notions of Jewish nationality and the concept of a Jewish State. His interpretations of Jewish law set him at odds with the increasing population of immigrant Jews from eastern Europe, and the latter part of his life was dogged by conflict.

Nathan Marcus Adler
Chief Rabbi
1803–1890

Nathan Marcus Adler was born in Hanover. His father was Mordecai Baer Adler, unofficial chief rabbi of the city. His mother's name remains unknown. Adler attended a series of universities and was awarded a PhD from Erlangen in 1828. In the same year he studied for the rabbinate and was ordained. In 1829 he was appointed *Landesrabbiner* (chief rabbi) of Oldenburg and then his native Hanover. Hanover was at that time under British control, and in 1844 Adler succeeded Solomon Hirschell as rabbi of the Great Synagogue at Duke's Place in London. He asserted his authority at every turn, refusing to let other rabbis use their own titles in his Beth Din (ecclesiastical court). In 1847 he consolidated the status of his office in his *Laws and Regulations for All the Synagogues in the United Kingdom*. He made sweeping reforms that resulted, in 1870, in the union of all the major Ashkenazi congregations in London into one United Synagogue. Adler believed in educational reform also. He campaigned tirelessly for more Jewish day schools, and it was under his authority that Jews' College was established in 1855.

Samuel Alexander

First Jewish Oxbridge Fellow
1859–1938

Samuel Alexander was born
in Sydney, Australia to
father Samuel Alexander and
South African mother Eliza
Sloman. In 1877 Alexander
left his family and set sail
for England, a voyage that
lasted 108 days. In England, Alexander was given a scholarship
to study philosophy at Balliol College, Oxford. After graduating,
he was awarded a fellowship at Lincoln College, Oxford. This
marked the first time that a Jew had been elected to a fellowship
at either Oxford or Cambridge. In 1893 Alexander began
his 31-year career at the University of Manchester, where he
was a popular and charismatic teacher. He supported various
university causes, including the campaign to provide residences
for female students. He was an early supporter of Zionism and
was responsible for introducing his friend Chaim Weizmann to
the politician Arthur Balfour. In 1920 Alexander's *Space, Time and
Deity* was published to wide acclaim. The work detailed his theory
that space and time occupy one metaphysical level from which
mind, time and matter emerge; he was considered one of the
greatest speculative thinkers of his time. In 1925 he was honoured
by the presentation of his bust by Jacob Epstein to the University
of Manchester.

Petrus Alfonsi

Transmitted Arabic knowledge
to the Latin Christian world
fl. 1106–1126

Petrus Alfonsi, originally Moses
Sephardi, was born in northern
Spain to Jewish parents but was
baptised a Christian when he
was 45. He was fluent in Hebrew
and Arabic. Sometime between
1110 and 1116 he emigrated to England, where he taught astronomy
and produced his astronomical tables. According to one manuscript
from Alfonsi's *Disciplina Clericalis*, he also served as royal physician to
King Henry I of England during this time. He then moved to northern
France and wrote the *Epistola ad Peripateticos in Francia* (*Letter
to the Peripatetics in France*). He became famous as a writer, and
wrote two major literary works. The first, the *Dialogi Contra Judaeos*
(*Dialogue Against the Jews*), a set of conversations between Alfonsi's
converted Christian self and his old Jewish self, became the most
widely read anti-Jewish text of the Latin Middle Ages. The second
work, the *Disciplina Clericalis* (*A Training-school for the Clergy*), was a
collection of proverbs that was translated into European vernaculars
and influenced Chaucer. Despite denying his Jewishness in the *Dialogi*,
Alfonsi shared the interests of many Jewish scholars of his time, in
theology, astronomy and mathematics, and helped to pass on this
knowledge to the Christian world.

Benjamin Artom
Rabbi
1835–1879

Benjamin Artom was born in Asti, Piedmont, Italy. His father was Elia Artom. Artom trained as a rabbi, held a number of rabbinical posts around Italy and was the first rabbi of Naples. In 1866 he was appointed haham (chief rabbi) of the Spanish and Portuguese Jews in London. This congregation was the oldest in London, and it worshipped at the imposing Bevis Marks synagogue. On his arrival Artom knew no English and delivered his first sermon in French, but by 1873 his grasp of the language was so accomplished that his sermons were published in book form. During the 1850s and 1860s the major Ashkenazi synagogues in London were contemplating amalgamation under the leadership of the Ashkenazi chief rabbi Nathan Marcus Adler. Artom managed the balancing act of resisting such pressure and maintaining the independence of his community, while maintaining good relations with the Ashkenazim. In 1870 he agreed to consecrate a new synagogue erected by Dutch Jews in the City of London, after Nathan Adler had refused to do so, and in 1872 did the same for the first Sephardi synagogue in Manchester. In 1877 he agreed to accept converts into Sephardi Judaism in England, further demonstrating the independence of the Spanish and Portuguese Jews in his adopted country.

Alfred Ayer

He declared a belief in God
to be meaningless
1910–1989

Alfred Ayer was born in
London to Jules Ayer, a Swiss
businessman, and his Dutch-
Jewish wife Reine Citroën, of
the Citroën car dynasty. Alfred
graduated in 1932 with a
first in classics from Christ Church College, Oxford. He spent the
next year in Vienna, where he attended lectures by philosopher
Moritz Shlick and the Vienna Circle. He returned to England in
1933 to take up his first lectureship. In 1936, at the age of 26,
Ayer's best-known work, *Language, Truth and Logic* was published,
making him the *enfant terrible* of British philosophy. Ayer's book
was the first English exposition on logical positivism. It argued that
all concepts can be separated into two categories: the verifiable
and the unverifiable. Verifiable ideas include those which can be
observed and those supported by logic. Unverifiable statements
however, such as the belief in God, cannot be supported by sense
experience and are thus meaningless. In line with his academic
beliefs, Ayer was not religious. During the Second World War,
he served with MI6 and the Special Operations Executive. Ayer
received a knighthood in 1970.

Leo Baeck

Rabbi, scholar and theologian
1873–1956

Born in Lisa, Germany (now Leszno in Poland), Leo Baeck was educated at the Jewish Theological Seminary of Breslau and the University of Berlin. He served as a rabbi while lecturing at Berlin's Higher Institute for Jewish Studies between 1913 and 1942. By this time Baeck had become a leading religious and public figure thanks to his 1905 work *The Essence of Judaism*. In 1933 he became president of the Reich Representation of German Jews, which aimed to support families of Jewish professionals who had been dismissed following antisemitic legislation. By 1941 Baeck was compelled to participate in mass deportations to the east, until his own deportation to Theresienstadt in 1943. There he held a protected position as an intermediary between guards and other prisoners. Though praised by survivors for his lectures on philosophy and religion, his decision not to reveal to inmates their likely fate has been much criticised. After liberation in 1945, Baeck settled in London and became president of the North Western Reform Synagogue and the World Union for Progressive Judaism. His second major work, *This People Israel*, was published in 1955, a year that also saw the founding of the Leo Baeck Institute, an international research institute for the study of German-speaking Jewry, with Baeck himself serving as its first president. Leo Baeck College, a progressive rabbinical seminary, was founded in Finchley, London in 1956.

Michael Balint
Psychoanalyst
1896–1970

Michael Balint was born Mihaly Bergsmann in Budapest, into an assimilated Hungarian family. At secondary school Balint became a voracious reader and haunted the libraries of Budapest. He harboured ambitions to be an engineer but his doctor father disapproved and in 1913 had him enrol, instead, in medical school. On the outbreak of the First World War he was conscripted into the army. In 1919, inspired by Sigmund Freud's *Totem and Taboo*, Balint attended courses in psychoanalysis, finishing his doctorate in 1920. In 1926 he established a psychoanalysis practice, publishing papers on bacteriology and biochemistry. Under an increasingly difficult political situation from 1932–8 all Jewish analysts were advised to leave Hungary, so Balint and his family settled in Manchester. In 1945 he received the news that his parents, under threat of arrest by Hungarian Nazis, had both committed suicide by lethal injection. Balint became a naturalised British subject in 1947, and in 1948 he was awarded an MSc in psychology by the University of Manchester. In the same year he took up a post at the Tavistock Clinic in north London, where he remained until his retirement in 1961. Balint gave his name to a number of significant theories pertaining to mother–infant relationships, including "primary love" (1952) and the "basic fault" (1968). He was also interested in the doctor–patient relationship; his classic work *The Doctor, his Patient and the Illness* (1957) stressed the psychological importance of what might be called the "bedside manner" over clinical treatment.

Lionel Barnett

World expert on ancient
Indian history and wisdom
1871–1960

Lionel Barnett was born in
Liverpool to banker Baron
Barnett and his wife Adele. As
a student at Cambridge he
studied classics and won many
student awards, including three
Sir William Browne's medals for Latin and Greek poetry. In 1899 he
joined the British Museum and became keeper for the Department
of Oriental Books and Manuscripts. He was responsible for
significantly extending the museum's collection and compiling
lengthy descriptive catalogues related to ancient Indian literature.
He was appointed to a professorship of Sanskrit at University
College London and published widely on Indian history, language
and culture. His famous *The Wisdom of the East* series is an example
of the many introductory texts he wrote for a general audience.
In 1950 he was awarded the Gold Medal of the Royal Asiatic
Society. He was an active member of his local Jewish community
and chaired a number of committees. He dedicated the last 12
years of his life to working for his old department at the British
Museum, even when his sight was failing him.

Richard David Barnett

Museum curator and
archaeologist
1909–1986

Richard Barnett was born
in Acton, west London. His
father Lionel Barnett was the
keeper of Oriental Printed
Books and Manuscripts at the
British Museum. Barnett was
educated at St Paul's School, Corpus Christi College, Cambridge
and the British School of Archaeology in Athens. He took up a
post at the British Museum and became Keeper of the Department
of Western Asiatic Antiquities. He produced books and catalogues
of the holdings at the British Museum and the Jewish Museum in
London. He was appointed a fellow of the British Academy and
received a CBE in 1974 for his services to scholarship. He received
an award in Israel for services to archaeology in the Bible lands.
Barnett was closely connected to the Bevis Marks Spanish and
Portuguese Synagogue, where he was a member, an elder and its
honorary archivist. He edited a book on its religious treasures and
a book of essays on Sephardi heritage. He served as President
of the Jewish Historical Society of England, Vice-Chairman of
the Jewish Museum in London and Chairman of the Anglo-Israel
Archaeological Society.

Peter Thomas Bauer

Development economist
who opposed overseas aid
1915–2002

Peter Thomas Bauer was born
in Budapest, Hungary, the
son of a bookmaker. He was
educated at the Scholae Piae
before moving to Britain in 1934,
where he read economics at
Gonville and Caius College, Cambridge. In 1939 he joined Guthrie
& Company, a London-based company with interests in rubber
and trading in the Middle East. After briefly working for the private
sector, in 1947 Bauer began his academic career as a lecturer in
agricultural economics at London University. In 1948 he became
a lecturer in economics at Cambridge, and in 1956 became Smuts
Reader in Commonwealth Studies. In 1960 he became a professor
at the London School of Economics. Bauer made significant
contributions to development economics, international development
and foreign aid. He was famously opposed to the idea of overseas
aid, which he believed obstructed development, and elaborated
on his ideas in his publications *The Economics of Underdeveloped
Countries* (1957), *Dissent on Development* (1976), *Equality, the Third
World and Economic Delusion* (1981) and *Reality and Rhetoric: Studies
in Economic Development* (1984). In 1982 Bauer was made a life
peer by Margaret Thatcher. Though born a Jew, he converted to
Catholicism in later life.

Zygmunt Bauman
Attempted to rationalise the
Holocaust through modernity
1925–2017

Zygmunt Bauman, a sociologist
and philosopher, was born in
Poznań, Poland to non-observant
Jewish parents. The family fled
the invading Nazis in 1939 and
relocated to the Soviet Union,
where Bauman became a communist. He studied sociology at Warsaw
University, where he later became a lecturer before departing in
1968 to escape a growing campaign of antisemitism in Poland.
Bauman first relocated to Tel-Aviv University in Israel before moving
to England, where he became Chair of Sociology at the University
of Leeds. There he produced his best-known and arguably his most
controversial work: *Modernity and the Holocaust* (1989), in which he
made the case that the Holocaust could be understood through a
framework of modern bureaucracy and rationalisation, and therefore
was an atrocity that modern societies should seek to understand.
He was a prolific academic and his publications on topics including
morality, consumerism, postmodernity and globalisation have become
key texts in various academic fields. He was an outspoken critic of
globalisation and Zionism and in 2011 he implied that the Israeli
treatment of Palestinians was akin to the Holocaust, comparing
the West Bank barrier in Israel to the Warsaw Ghetto. Bauman won
numerous prizes throughout his career and in 2010 the University
of Leeds established the Bauman Institute within the School of
Sociology and Social Policy in his honour.

Max Beloff

Historian, political
scientist and life peer
1913–1999

Max Beloff was born in Islington,
London. His parents had
emigrated from Russia to Britain
in 1903. He was educated at
King Alfred School in Hampstead,
St Paul's School, London and
Corpus Christi College, Oxford. As Nuffield Reader in Oxford he
published many books on American themes. His book *The American
Federal Government* became a standard text of its time. He also wrote
books on Soviet foreign policy and on European history. As a fellow
at All Souls, Oxford he concentrated on American foreign policy
in relation to Europe, and British foreign policy during the passing
of the British Empire. This endeavour, among other publications,
resulted in his two-volume study *Imperial Sunset, 1897–1942*. Later
he became deeply involved in politics and also campaigned for
the founding of the University College of Buckingham, of which he
became principal. He believed that universities should be private
initiatives that operate outside of the state-financed framework to
avoid control and retain autonomy. He received a knighthood in 1980
and a peerage in 1981. He identified as a Jew, played a role in Jewish
academic institutions such as the Wiener Library and was a loyal but
critical Zionist. He was deeply grateful for the opportunities life in
England gave him. He changed political allegiances more than once
and was an outspoken Eurosceptic.

JEWISH SCHOOL AND FAMILY BIBLE

A. (ABRAHAM) BENISCH   Volume 1

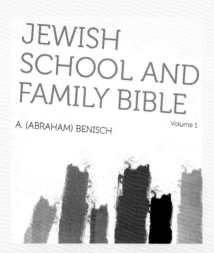

Abraham Benisch
Hebraist and journalist
1811–1878

Abraham Benisch was a journalist and Jewish social campaigner. He was born in Bohemia and studied at the University of Prague, where he formed a student group that campaigned for Jewish independence in Palestine. After moving to Vienna, Benisch continued in his venture, forming a secret society in order to further the mission of restoring Jewish independence in the Holy Land. Benisch moved to London in 1841, seeking the support for his cause from prominent British Jews. After failing to get a positive response to his proposals he turned to the world of journalism. In 1854 he purchased the *Hebrew Observer*, which he later merged with the *Jewish Chronicle*. Benisch oversaw the growth of the paper and used it as a mouthpiece for many of his social ideas. He campaigned for the admission of Jews into parliament and against forced conversion to Christianity abroad. Benisch helped found several learned societies, including the Biblical Institute and the Syro-Egyptian and the Biblical Chronological societies. He was also an active member of the Jewish community, helping to establish the Jewish Board of Guardians, the Anglo-Jewish Association and the Society for Hebrew Literature. His published works included An *Elementary Hebrew Grammar* (1852) and *Manual of Scripture History* (1863).

Menasseh ben Israel

Rabbi and readmission
campaigner
1604–1657

Menasseh ben Israel was born
in Portugal. His parents Joseph
(ben Israel) Soeiro and Rachel
Abranel were Marranos (secret
Jews). The family emigrated to
Amsterdam while Menasseh was
still a child. In 1622 he was appointed rabbi of one of Amsterdam's
three synagogues. He established the city's first Hebrew printing
house, and his most famous early work was *Conciliador,* a
commentary on the Old Testament that was notable in that it did
not attack Christianity. Such a neutral stance served him well, and
he became the unofficial ambassador of western Jewry to European
Christendom. Ben Israel launched a campaign for the readmission
of Jews to England and was given a passport and permission to visit
in 1655. On 31 October he formally submitted a petition to the
council of state. It had the unforeseen consequence of revealing the
presence of several secret communities of Jews in England, who were
left with little choice but to throw themselves on the mercy of the
Lord Protector. On 24 March 1656 Ben Israel famously presented
his petition to Oliver Cromwell himself. Cromwell fell short of
formally answering it, instead turning a blind eye to the presence
of the Jews in England. Ben Israel was personally granted a pension
by Cromwell, but surrendered it in return for financial help to return
the body of his recently deceased son Samuel to the Netherlands.

Herbert Bentwich

Lawyer and Zionist leader
1856–1932

Herbert Bentwich was born
in Whitechapel, London.
His parents were Mattathias
Bentwich, a Polish jeweller, and
his wife Rosa. A sickly child,
Bentwich was educated at
Woodman's, a Christian-run
school in London's Bishopsgate, then at a Jewish boarding school
in Edmonton and lastly at the Whitechapel Foundation. In 1872
Bentwich enrolled at University College London. Graduating with
honours in 1877, he set up in practice as a solicitor in the city of
London. Specialising in copyright law, he became a barrister and
was admitted to the Inner Temple in 1903. He began to practice
on the south-eastern circuit, but preferred his editorial of the *Law
Journal,* a periodical he owned, to being in court. In 1875 Bentwich
undertook voluntary work for the Jewish Board of Guardians. It was
a beginning of a lifetime of active involvement in Jewish communal
affairs, which included posts at Jews' College, the St John's Wood
synagogue and the Stepney Jewish schools. In 1892 he helped found
Hampstead Synagogue. Bentwich was a passionate Zionist, wedded
to the Chovevei Zion ("Lovers of Zion") philosophy. He founded the
Maccabeans along with the artist Solomon Joseph Solomon, brother
of his wife Susannah. In 1897 he led 21 Jewish "pilgrims", including
Israel Zangwill, to Palestine. Bentwich took a prominent role,
alongside Nahum Sokolow and Chaim Weizmann, in the negotiations
that led to the Balfour Declaration of 1917.

Isaiah Berlin

Philosopher and
historian of ideas
1909–1997

Isaiah Berlin was born in Riga,
Latvia to Mendel Berlin and his
wife Marie. Berlin's parents were
secular Jews but his wider family
was devout. The Berlins moved
to Petrograd but were caught up
in the antisemitism of the Russian Revolution and moved to England.
Berlin was educated at St Paul's School in London and at Corpus
Christi College Oxford. In 1932 he became the first Jew to be elected
to a fellowship at All Souls. He took a lectureship in philosophy,
where his inspirational style and oratorial skills influenced generations
of students. In 1939 he wrote a celebrated biography of Karl Marx.
On the outbreak of the Second World War Berlin was invited back
to Russia by his friend Guy Burgess. He only made it as far as New
York, and saw out the war in the US. In 1953 he wrote *The Hedgehog
and the Fox*, his major work on Tolstoy's theory of history. In 1966
he consolidated his academic credentials by becoming the president
of Wolfson College Oxford. Berlin was a prolific author, his work
spanning the range of social and political theory, philosophy and
the history of ideas. Berlin was a liberal Zionist who was enthusiastic
about the creation of Israel. He was knighted in 1957, and appointed
to the Order of Merit in 1971.

Basil Bernstein

Explored the relationship
between class and
communication
1924–2000

Basil Bernstein was born in the
East End of London to Jewish
immigrant parents. Although
he was underage, Bernstein
managed to volunteer for
the RAF during the Second World War and served in Africa as
a bombardier. On demobilisation, he worked with the Stepney
settlement boys' club, which he would later cite as a formative
experience for his development of sociolinguistics. Bernstein went
to the London School of Economics in 1947 to study sociology
and, after training at Kingsway Day College, he began teaching
classes at the City Day College, in Shoreditch. He joined University
College London in 1960 and studied linguistics and phonetics
before gaining his PhD. He was made head of the sociological
research unit at the Institute of Education in 1967. There he
produced his most groundbreaking research, demonstrating the
relationship between class and communication and the implications
for learning. He suggested that children from a poorer background
often developed a restricted code of speaking that held them
back at school. Initially his work attracted considerable criticism,
often due to misunderstanding or misinterpretation of it. Its
later developments, however, have gone on to exert considerable
influence in the fields of both pedagogy and linguistics.

Max Black
He believed in a dynamic
approach to philosophy
1909–1988

Max Black was born in modern-
day Azerbaijan to Lionel Black
and Sophia Davinska. The family
moved to England in 1912 to
escape antisemitic persecution.
While studying mathematics
at Queens' College Cambridge, Black attended lectures given by
the celebrated philosopher Wittgenstein. He graduated in 1930
and began teaching in Newcastle-upon-Tyne. He later lectured
in mathematics at the Institute of Education in London, before
moving to the United States to teach philosophy. Black became
frustrated with the rigidity of philosophical thought and instead
argued that ideas benefited from freedom of reflection and
approaches taken from different philosophical schools. He also
strongly believed that philosophy could treat the ills of society. A
prolific writer, he made contributions to the philosophy of language,
the philosophy of mathematics and science and the philosophy
of art. His major work, *A Companion to Wittgenstein's Tractatus*, was
instrumental in the understanding of his former teacher's ideas.
Black was an accomplished chess player and also enjoyed playing
ping-pong. Although he was not observant, he seriously considered
moving to Israel, where he had lectured throughout his career.

Lionel Blue

The first openly gay
British rabbi
1930–2016

Rabbi Lionel Blue was born
in London's East End to
parents of Russian ancestry.
He lost his faith at the age
of five when God failed
to intervene and remove
Hitler and Mosley. After returning to religion at university, Blue
was ordained as a rabbi in 1960. In 1980, he became the first
British rabbi to come out as gay. In the 1960s Blue was minister
at various synagogues and was appointed European director
for the World Union of Progressive Judaism. He was a regular
speaker on BBC Radio 4's *Thought for the Day*, and his radio and
occasional TV appearances made him a well-known and popular
figure among Jews and non-Jews alike. He authored a number of
works including *Godly and Gay* (1981) and *The Godseeker's Guide*
(2010). Lionel Blue claimed that when he returned to Judaism
he "fell in love with love", becoming a much happier person. His
jokes, on both Jewish and non Jewish subjects, were legendary. He
believed in a personal God, whom he named Fred. He was awarded
the OBE in 1994.

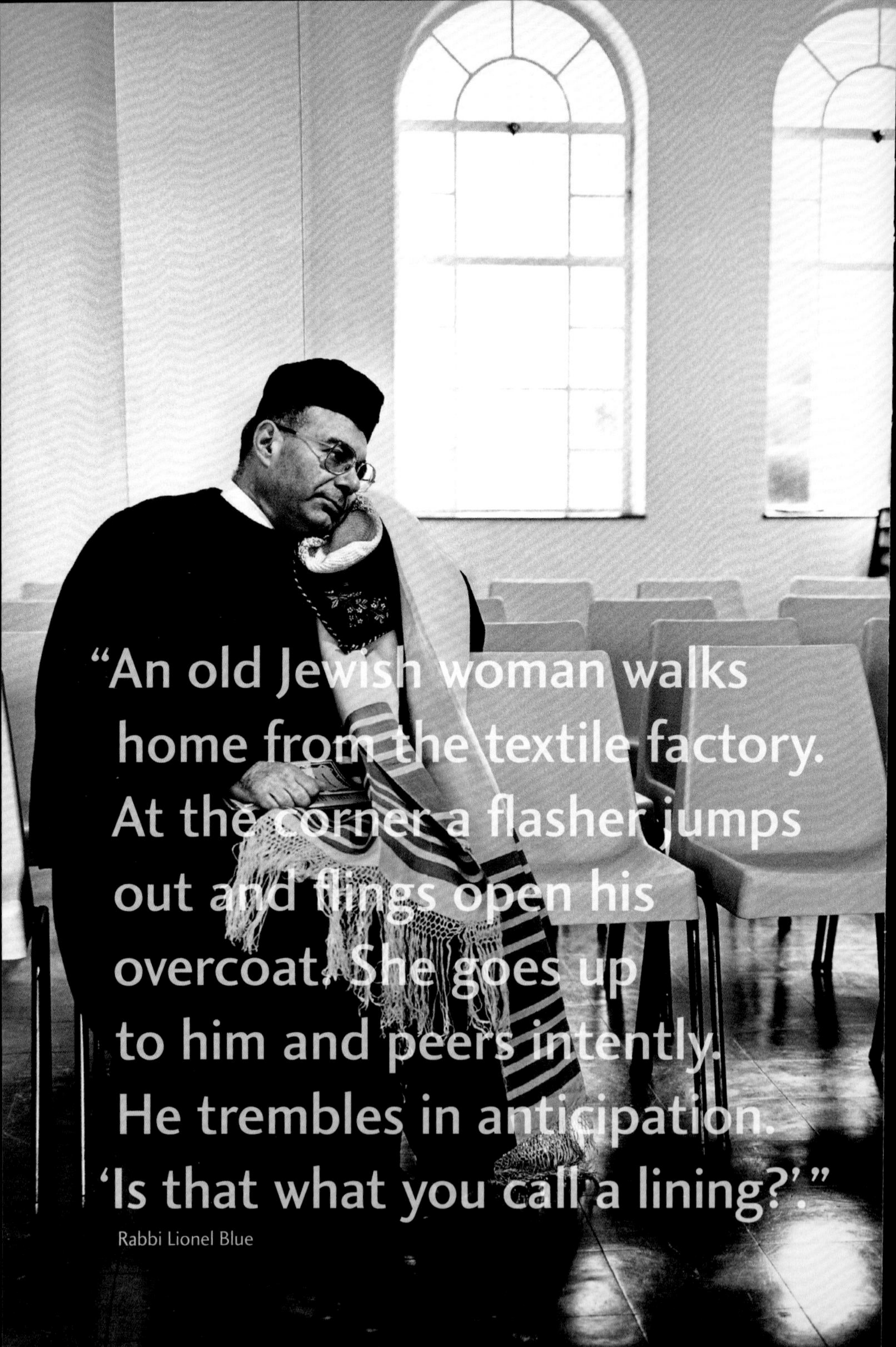

"An old Jewish woman walks
home from the textile factory.
At the corner a flasher jumps
out and flings open his
overcoat. She goes up
to him and peers intently.
He trembles in anticipation.
'Is that what you call a lining?'."

Rabbi Lionel Blue

Israel Brodie

Chief Rabbi

1895–1979

Israel Brodie was born in Newcastle-upon-Tyne. He was the son of Aaron Uri Brodie, a sales rep from Kovno, and Sheina Maggid. He was educated at Rutherford College, Newcastle, and in 1912 he was enrolled in both University College London and Jews' College London to train in the Jewish ministry. After taking a first in 1915, he headed to Balliol College, Oxford to work for a B.Litt on the origins of Karaism. From 1917 to 1919 he served as a chaplain on the Western Front. After the war he took formal rabbinical training, and was ordained in 1923. In the same year he went to Melbourne to become the rabbi there. He returned to England in 1937, first to Balliol, then to his *alma mater* Jews' College where he became a tutor and lecturer. The Second World War intervened, and in 1944 Brodie became senior Jewish chaplain to the British Army (aka the Forces Rabbi). In 1946 he returned to Jews' College once more, this time to serve as its president. In 1948 he was appointed Chief Rabbi, and served until 1965 when he became the first incumbent to retire. A committed Zionist, he visited Israel frequently. There he supported the creation of both the secular University of Jerusalem and the religious Bar Ilan University, where a chair was named in his honour. Brodie's major scholarly work was the publication of the *Etz Hayyim* of the 13th-century Jewish figure Jacob of London. He was knighted for services to British Jewry and appointed to the Order of the Companion of Honour.

Felix Falk Carlebach

Rabbi and orator

1911–2008

Felix Falk Carlebach was born in Lubeck, Germany. He was the son of Simson Carlebach, a banker, and his wife Resi, née Graupe. He was educated at Katharineum zu Lubeck, then studied music and theology in Cologne. In 1939, thanks to the special visas arranged by Chief Rabbi Joseph Herz's religious emergency council, he and his wife were brought to Britain from Germany. Thus, Carlebach escaped the fate of his parents, who were deported and killed. He later said, "It was one of the luckiest events of my life that my wife and I survived." In 1941, due to many Jewish ministers being called up as wartime chaplains, Carlebach was placed at Palmers Green and Southgate United Synagogue. There he developed a reputation as a fine orator in his adopted language of English, always retaining his distinctive German-Jewish accent. It was said of him that having Carlebach speak one's funeral oration would almost make dying worthwhile. In 1947 he was appointed minister of the South Manchester Synagogue, a position he held until his retirement 40 years later. During his tenure he served as chaplain to the Lord Mayors of Manchester, and was Vice-President of the Council of Christians and Jews. Carlebach was Orthodox in his views, without being evangelical about them. He was a great music lover, and was a familiar figure at the concerts of Manchester's famous Hallé orchestra. Since 1983 the orchestra has given an annual concert in Carlebach's name.

Eli Cashdan
Rabbi and chaplain
1905–1998

Eli Cashdan was born in Starye Dorogi, Minsk, in modern-day Belarus. His parents were Joseph and Bessie Cashdan. When he was three months old, he came to Britain with his mother and four siblings to join his father, who was working in Liverpool as a rabbi and shohet. He studied at the Liverpool Yeshiva and was ordained at the very young age of 17. He went on to London University and Jews' College, where he took a first-class degree in Semitics. He was called to the bar at London's Lincoln's Inn in 1933. In 1941 Cashdan joined the Royal Air Force, where he served as Senior Jewish Chaplain, and was discharged in 1946 with the rank of wing commander. Cashdan took up a post as headmaster of local Hebrew classes in Hove, then in 1950 was appointed Senior Lecturer at Jews' College, where he remained until his retirement in 1975. Cashdan was a well-respected scholar, and worked for the Soncino Press, contributing to their *Soncino Books of the Bible* series. He wrote a new translation for the centenary edition of the Singer prayer book, published in 1990. His new translation of the Psalms (1997) was described by Chief Rabbi Lord Jonathan Sacks as allowing "these masterpieces of religion to speak their ageless power to a new generation".

David Cesarani
Historian and broadcaster
1956–2015

David Cesarani was born in London to Henry Cesarani and Sylvia Packman. He was educated at Latymer Upper School in Hammersmith, Queens' College Cambridge, Columbia University New York and St Antony's College Oxford. He held posts at the Universities of Leeds, Southampton and Manchester, the Wiener Library and at Royal Holloway, University of London, where he was Research Professor of Jewish History. He was a leading British expert on modern Anglo-Jewish history and the Holocaust and authored 15 books. He also edited and co-edited several collections of essays, such as *The Making of Modern Anglo-Jewry*, which showcased the work of a new group of historians who, like himself, sought to present the British-Jewish relationship without being bound by the celebratory or deferential manner of the past. He played a major role in researching, writing and speaking about the Holocaust and helped to shape the War Crimes Act (1991) and to establish Holocaust Memorial Day in 2001. In 2005 Cesarini was awarded an OBE for his services to Holocaust education. He believed in Israel's right to exist and supported a two-state solution. On holiday, David would often follow the route taken by Jews fleeing from occupied France crossing the Pyrenees.

Tony Cliff

Leader of Socialist
Workers Party
1917–2000

Tony Cliff was born Yigael
Gluckstein. He grew up in
British Mandatory Palestine. In
his youth he joined a socialist-
Zionist group but quickly
came to oppose Zionism as
a nationalist movement that pitted workers against one another.
He became a Trotskyist, and his membership of the proscribed
Revolutionary Communist League led in 1939 to his imprisonment
for a year. In 1945 he married Chanie Rosenberg, a South African
socialist, and the two moved to London in 1947. Rosenberg's British
citizenship allowed her husband to become a resident, though he
remained stateless for the rest of his life. In London Cliff threw
himself into politics and in 1950 helped found the Socialist Review
Group, which in 1962 would become the International Socialists,
and in 1977 the Socialist Workers Party (SWP), with Cliff as its
effective leader. During these years Cliff became a leading voice
within Trotskyism, arguing that the Soviet system was one of state
capitalism with which revolutionaries should break completely. This
stance made the SWP more intellectually attractive than most rival
parties and helped to explain its endurance since the revolutions
of 1989–91 (which the SWP welcomed). When Cliff died in 2000
he was remembered for his warmth as well as his zeal. His most
significant books include *Lenin* (four volumes, 1975–79), *Trotsky*
(four volumes, 1989–93) and the memoir *A World To Win* (2000).

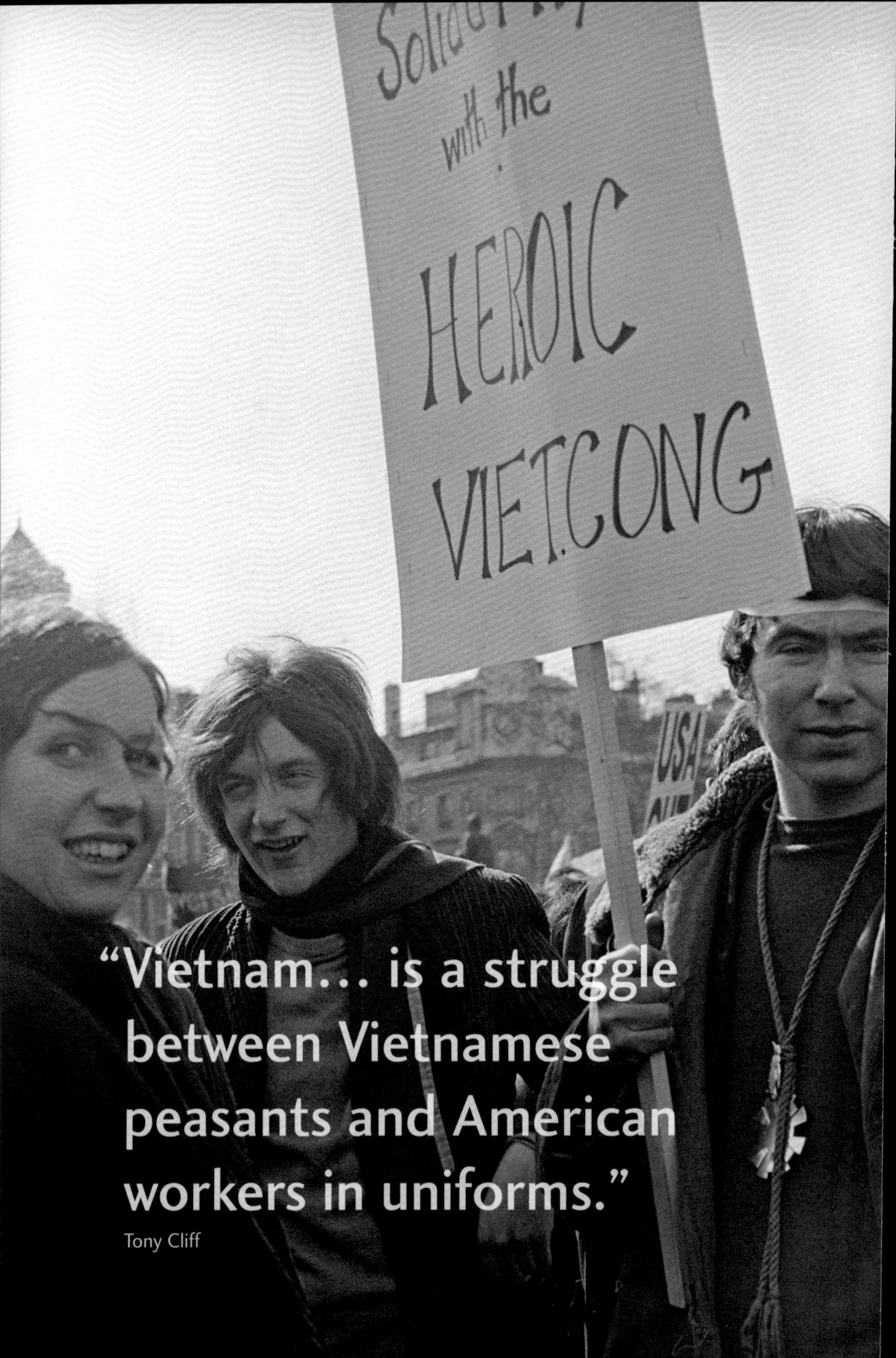

Solidarity with the **HEROIC VIETCONG**

USA

"Vietnam… is a struggle between Vietnamese peasants and American workers in uniforms."

Tony Cliff

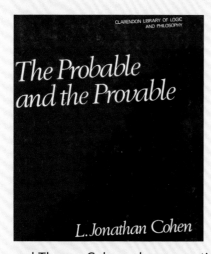

Laurence Jonathan Cohen

He showed the everyday application of philosophy

1923–2006

Laurence Jonathan Cohen made contributions to numerous disciplines including law, psychology and political thought. He was born to Israel and Theresa Cohen, who were active in the World Zionist Movement. He was educated in London and then at Balliol College Oxford. The Second World War interrupted his university education and Cohen first trained as a code-breaker at Bletchley Park. Later, after having learned Japanese, he served as an intelligence officer in the Far East. Throughout his academic career he held several posts at the University of Oxford. His major works include *The Principles of World Citizenship*, which examined international law and duty, and *The Diversity of Meaning*, which explored the concept of nature. His most famous book, *The Probable and the Provable* (1977), criticised the theory of probability put forward by 17th-century philosopher Blaise Pascal; Cohen argued that there are different forms of probability, not just one. This led to groundbreaking discussions among philosophers but also within Britain's legal system. Cohen was committed to his faith and he invited his students to share lively Passover dinners with his family.

Chapman Cohen

Established materialism as
the philosophy of Atheism
1868–1954

Chapman Cohen was born
in Leicester, the oldest son
of Enoch Cohen, a Jewish
confectioner, and his wife,
Deborah Barnett. Cohen stated
that he had "little religion at
home and none at school". He attended a local elementary school
but was otherwise self-educated. In 1890 a chance encounter with
a Christian Evidence lecturer in Victoria Park, which resulted in him
challenging the speaker, led to an invitation to lecture from the local
Secular Society. Some months later he joined the National Secular
Society and he was soon in high demand, giving over 200 lectures a
year. In 1898, he became Assistant Editor of G. W. Foote's *Freethinker*
and in 1915, following Foote's death, he was appointed its editor.
He rose, too, to become the president of the National Secular
Society. Cohen was a prolific writer on secularism, and published
over 50 works including *A Grammar of Freethought* (1921), *Theism or
Atheism* (1921) and *Materialism Restated* (1927). His views achieved
a wide public audience when he debated "Materialism: has it been
exploded?" with C. E. M. Joad at the Caxton Hall, Westminster, in
1928. He resigned as president of the society in 1949, but remained
editor of the *Freethinker* until his retirement in 1951.

Gerald Cohen

The inspiration behind the
Non-Bullshit Marxism Group
1941–2009

Gerald Cohen was a political
philosopher. Born in Montreal
to factory workers Morrie and
Bella Cohen, he was raised in a
secular, communist household.
After graduating from McGill
University, Cohen studied philosophy at New College, Oxford, where
he met Isaiah Berlin. In 1978 he published his best known work, *Karl
Marx's Theory of History: A Defence.* He advocated analytical Marxism,
an examination of Marxist ideas through the application of logic
and rational enquiry. The book was hailed as the best explanation
of Marxist theory written to date and it inspired the foundation
of the *September Group* (also known as the Non-Bullshit Marxism
Group), which sought to further promote his academic approach.
Cohen published more works, including *If You're Egalitarian, How
Come You're So Rich?* in which he examined what political principles
imply for the personal behaviour of those who subscribe to them
and how egalitarian principals are a matter of personal attitude and
choice. Cohen was close friends with fellow Jewish Marxist scholar
Marshall Berman. Although raised in a secular household, where his
barmitzvah consisted of reading aloud a Yiddish story, Cohen came
to have a firm appreciation for Jewish tradition.

Stanley Cohen

Sociologist and criminologist
1942–2013

Stanley Cohen was born in Johannesburg, South Africa. His father was Ray Cohen, a businessman who had emigrated from Lithuania, and his mother was Sie, the daughter of Polish immigrants. Cohen attended Parktown Boys' High School, and then went on to study at the University of Witwatersrand. In the early 1960s he moved to London, where he worked as a psychiatric worker from 1963 to 1964 before studying at the London School of Economics. There he read for a PhD on hooligans, vandals and the community. Cohen went on to have a distinguished academic career lecturing at Enfield College (1965–7), the University of Durham (1967–72) and, from 1972, the University of Essex. In the early 1980s Cohen moved to Israel, where he became Professor of Criminology at the Hebrew University of Jerusalem. He later admitted that he had idealised his image of life in Israel, claiming in 2001 that moving there had been a "mistake". He did, however, become actively involved in the human rights movement, writing a 1991 report that documented the torture and ill-treatment of Palestinian prisoners during the intifada. His book *States of Denial,* in which he investigated social reaction to human rights abuses, won the British Academy book prize in 2002. In the mid-1990s Cohen returned to London, and his *alma mater* the London School of Economics, this time as Visiting Centennial Professor (1994–5).

Norman Cohn

Historian, linguist and Fellow
of the British Academy
1915–2007

Norman Cohn was born in
London to a Jewish father and
a Catholic mother. He was
educated at Gresham's School
and Christ Church, Oxford. He
is best known for his book *The
Pursuit of the Millennium,* which was translated into a dozen languages
and ranked as one of the 100 most influential books of the 20th
century by the *Times Literary Supplement.* It sets out parallels between
the apocalyptic beliefs that fuelled medieval heresies and 20th-
century Nazi and communist Orthodoxies. In *Europe's Inner Demons,*
an influential historical study of beliefs on European witchcraft, he
again implies a continuance of the societal need for scapegoats.
As Director of the Columbus Centre for Studies of Persecution
and Genocide at the University of Sussex, he produced *Warrant for
Genocide,* examining the myth of the 'Jewish world conspiracy' in the
forged *The Protocols of the Elders of Zion* pamphlet. His book *Cosmos,
Chaos and the World to Come* examined humanity's inclination towards
'End of the World' beliefs, picking up, like his previous work, on the
theme of persecutorial fanaticism. Cohn had personal motives for
his research and books since many of his relatives had perished in
the Holocaust in Nazi Germany; he described all his work as studies
on the ideas and beliefs that aimed "to purify the world through the
annihilation of some category of human beings imagined as agents of
corruption and incarnations of evil".

"America is a mistake,
a gigantic mistake it is true,
but nonetheless a mistake."
Sigmund Freud

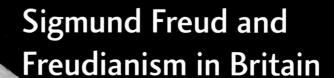

Sigmund Freud and Freudianism in Britain

In September 1909, during his only trip to America, Sigmund Freud visited Coney Island. Here he observed the most graphic manifestations of the American psyche. This leering demon, 'Funny Face', would have greeted him at the entrance to Steeplechase Park, the first of the three original parks built there.

In the Madhouse, from the series 'A Rake's Progress' by William Hogarth, 1832–34. In this final scene, having been driven mad by his own immorality, the subject of the series, Tom Rakewell, ends his days in Bedlam lunatic asylum. In the background the fashionably dressed women have come to be entertained by the bizarre antics of the inmates.

Sigmund Freud and Freudianism in Britain

Professor William D. Rubinstein
Historian and author

When in 1938 Sigmund Freud was forced by Nazism to emigrate,
he came to Britain, not to the United States or some other country.
While psychoanalysis was still viewed with deep suspicion in Britain,
to an unexpected and unusual extent it also flourished here in
positive soil. Of course, the treatment of persons deemed "insane"
or mentally ill pre-dated Freud and psychoanalysis by many centuries,
as did other modern forms of psychiatry, including approaches
that did not agree with Freudianism. The treatment of the insane
in "madhouses" such as Bedlam (St Mary Bethlehem, founded
as a hospital in 1330), with the public viewing of its inmates as
exhibitions, was a notorious feature of British society, as were other
"lunatic asylums" both public and private. The number of patients
held in asylums in Britain was, until surprisingly late, vast, with
no fewer than 150,000 patients in public and private asylums in
Britain in the 1950s. The professionalisation of the treatment of
mental illness began in 1841, with the formation of the Association
of Medical Officers of Asylums and Hospitals for the Insane, which,
via several changes of name, eventually became the Royal College
of Psychiatrists. (A "psychiatrist", it should be noted, is a medical
practitioner with an M.D. who specialises in mental illness or related
conditions; all psychiatrists are medically trained physicians.)

When Freudian psychoanalysis emerged at the beginning of the
20th century as a separate, highly influential but very controversial
sub-speciality of psychiatry in Britain, it thus did so in a society with

a well-established history of the treatment of mental illness, which was in the process of being professionalised as a medical speciality. Freudian psychoanalysis, however, presented many specific challenges in terms of its being fully accepted in Britain. With its uncompromising insistence on the centrality of sexuality in the human psyche, comprising such unsettling concepts as early childhood sexuality and the Oedipus Complex, it came into direct conflict with British Puritanism and the suppression of any frank explication of sexuality, especially unorthodox sexuality. For instance, in 1897 a bookseller was prosecuted for selling *Sexual Inversion*, a medical textbook (the first one ever published) on homosexuality by Havelock Ellis and John Addington Symonds. But on the other hand, Britain was also the home of a liberal intelligentsia comprised of upper- and upper-middle-class university graduates – of which the Bloomsbury Group is probably the best-known example – which was *de facto* allowed considerable leeway in its viewpoint and behaviour provided that these were not grossly offensive. It is also the case, and a salient point, that Freud and most (but not all) of his early followers were Jews, a fact that, on the Continent, far-right antisemites were keen to emphasise. The British situation, however, was significantly different from that of the Continent. Throughout central and eastern Europe, Jews comprised a very disproportionate percentage of local physicians, especially in major cities like Berlin, Vienna and Budapest. They also comprised a high and visible percentage of local bohemians, political radicals and cultural modernists. By contrast, in Britain the situation was very different. Only a tiny percentage of British physicians were Jews. Jews were also few and far between among Britain's radicals, who in any case were less numerous and less visible than on the Continent. These facts contributed to the surprisingly ready acceptance of Freud and Freudianism in Britain.

One under-appreciated fact about Sigmund Freud is that he was a lifelong anglophile. His half-brother lived in Manchester; Freud himself first came to England in 1875, when he was 19, to stay with him. This visit had a significant influence on his life. As a result, Freud developed what a biographer later described as an "insatiable appetite" for English literature. He was also strongly attracted to the English empiricist philosophers and thinkers. In 1879 or 1880 Freud was conscripted into the Austrian army – it is difficult to imagine Sigmund Freud as a soldier, but he was – and spent much of his time translating four essays by John Stuart Mill into German. Freud's lifelong Anglophilia made him highly sympathetic to British colleagues and admirers and was a significant factor in the later establishment of a Freudian network in Britain, as well as in his decision to move to London after the *Anschluss*. In contrast, Freud disliked the United States and American culture. In 1909, in the company of Carl Gustav Jung (then his heir apparent) and his Welsh disciple Ernest Jones, Freud visited America for the first and only time, a guest of G. Stanley Hall, the president of Clark University in Worcester, Massachusetts. Freud's dislike of America has been attributed to what he found on his trip, from bad cooking to the lack of public toilets, but at its heart was the European intellectual's prevalent view of the United States as vulgar, materialistic and devoid of high culture. (In New York, Freud and his entourage were taken on a visit to, of all places, Coney Island, the vast amusement park and public beach in Brooklyn, which was something like a giant Blackpool. Freud's visit to Coney Island sounds like a scene in a Woody Allen film, but it actually happened.) Thus, although by the 1930s the United States, and especially New York and Los Angeles, had become the most important locus of Freudian psychoanalysis, when Freud left Vienna it was to London that he came to live, not to New York.

Hamlet, Royal Shakespeare Company, 2008, Hamlet, David Tennant, prepares to kill Claudius, Patrick Stewart.

Sigmund Freud, Freud's psychoanalytic couch at the Freud Museum in London.

The most important British figure in establishing and popularising Freud's work in Britain was Ernest Jones (1879–1958), a Welsh neurologist from Gowerton near Swansea, who was educated at Cardiff University and at University College London. Jones had been influenced by Freud's writings from around 1905, although they did not meet until 1908. From then on, Jones became an intimate and acknowledged member of Freud's inner circle, sometimes described as his "Welsh wizard", the only English-speaking member of the inner circle and one of its few non-Jewish members. (Carl Gustav Jung was another, until he broke comprehensively with Freud and established a rival system of psychological explanation.) Freud's inner circle was well-defined and became a cult-like coterie, with its members given rings to prove their inclusion. While Jones's first wife, the Welsh composer and pianist Morfydd Llwyn Owen (1891–1918) was a Protestant, his second wife Katherine Joki, a friend of Freud's daughters, was Jewish, cementing further his membership in the inner circle. From 1913, Jones lived in London, where he founded the British Psychoanalytical Society and the International Psychoanalytical Association (serving as its president from 1920 to 1924 and 1932 to 1949) and was the founder and editor of the *International Journal of Psychoanalysis*. He was significant in the translation of many of Freud's works into English, and was the author of the first and best-known work that used Freudianism to interpret literature, *Hamlet and Oedipus* (1910 and 1949), which argued – needless to say controversially – that Hamlet's procrastination in killing Claudius was due to his having an Oedipus complex. After Freud's death, Jones wrote his seminal and distinguished three-volume biography, *Sigmund Freud: Life and Work* (1953, 1955 and 1957), which remains the most comprehensive account of his life. Jones's greatest service to Freud, however, was his instrumental role (assisted by Princess Marie Bonaparte and American ambassador to France William Bullitt) in bringing Freud and most of his family and entourage safely to London after the Nazi takeover. Jones had several well-placed friends in the British government who were able to facilitate their migration. Despite the controversial nature of his theories, the red carpet was rolled out for Freud in England. For instance, he was granted membership of the Royal Society, the celebrated scientific body. New fellows are required to attend a ceremony and sign its membership book. For the only time in its history, in Freud's case and in view of his age, the membership book was brought by the president and vice-presidents of the Society for Freud to sign at his home, a privilege previously reserved only for Royals made honorary fellows. This act was widely interpreted as reflecting the repugnance among British intellectuals for Nazi antisemitism. As is well-known, Freud spent the last 15 months of his life at 20 Maresfield Gardens, the house that was bought for him in Hampstead and is now the Freud Museum.

A second major source for the spread of Freud and his teachings in Britain was the Bloomsbury Group. After the First World War, several notable members of the Group became leading exponents of Freudianism, consistent with their long-standing interest in introspection and human emotion, and their frank discussions of sexuality. The most important figures connecting Freud, Bloomsbury and the wider public were James Strachey (1887–1967) and his wife Alix Sargant-Florence (1892–1973). James Strachey was the younger brother of Lytton Strachey (1880–1932), who was at the heart of the famous Group. At Cambridge, James had been an Apostle, a member of the famous secret society from which many Bloomsburies were recruited. Both James and his wife attended Bloomsbury salons in London. Already interested in Freud's work, shortly after their marriage in 1920 James and Alix moved to Vienna, where they were analysed by Freud. Back in England, they became members of the British Psychoanalytic Society and (at Freud's request) spent much of the period to about 1950 translating Freud's writings into English, as well as the works of other Continental Freudians. Between 1953 and 1966 they produced the 24 volumes of *The Standard Edition of the Complete Psychological Works of Sigmund Freud*, the most significant primary source of Freud's writings in English. It was James Strachey who translated Freud's German terms "Ich", "Es" and "Uber-Ich" as "Ego", "Id" and "Super-Ego" rather than their literal equivalents. The volumes of *The Standard Edition* were published by the Hogarth Press, the publishing firm founded in 1917 by Leonard and Virginia Woolf (and carried on after Virginia's death by Leonard Woolf and John Lehmann). Freudianism thus came to be at the heart of the Bloomsbury Group in its later phase.

After his death in 1939, and beyond the confines of Bloomsbury, Freud and his teachings had become a pervasive feature of British intellectual life. In the famous phrase of W. H. Auden, in his poem *In Memory of Sigmund Freud*, "to us he is no more a person/now but a whole climate of opinion/under whom we conduct our different lives". H. G. Wells predicted that Freud and Jung would take their places in history alongside Newton and Pasteur. As early as 1923, the *New Statesman* claimed that "We are all psychoanalysts now." Much of the cultural influence of Freud in England was, however, more subtle and indirect than in the United States, although by the time of his death Freud had become a universally known icon and seminal influence in British culture.

The third pathway by which Freudianism became significant in Britain was through other immigrant psychotherapists who were crucially influenced by Sigmund Freud. Perhaps the best known were his own daughter Anna Freud (1895–1982) and Melanie Klein

(1882–1960). Anna Freud came to London shortly after the arrival of her father in 1938; Melanie Klein migrated to London in 1926, at the invitation of Ernest Jones. Anna Freud and Melanie Klein had a famous extended dispute about the role of play and aggression among young children in which Klein, who (unlike Sigmund Freud) had extensive experience in observing young children, took issue with the Freuds, leading to a deep split in the British Psychoanalytical Association. Other very significant Continental psychotherapists who came to England, almost always because of Nazi or other persecution, included Erwin Stengel (1902–73), Michael Balint (1896–1970), Paula Heimann (1899–1982), Wilhelm ("Willy") Mayer-Gross (1889–1982) and many others. Although most refugee psychotherapists went to America, a major share went to London. There, they joined British-born psychotherapists, both Jewish and non-Jewish, such as David Eder (1895–1936) and Betty Joseph (1917–2013). Before the First World War, Eder had published the first English translations of works by both Freud and Jung and had influenced the novels of D. H. Lawrence. He was also a leading Zionist and served as president of the Zionist Federation of Great Britain. Jews also played an important role among British psychiatrists who were not wholly supportive of Freudian psychoanalysis, for example the important figures of the Australian-born Sir Aubrey Lewis (1900–75), the first Professor of Psychiatry at the Institute of Psychiatry, and Sir Martin Roth (1917–2006), Professor of Psychiatry at Cambridge University and the first president (1971–75) of the Royal College of Psychiatry. Even today, however, the Freudian-based British Psychoanalytical Society, and its related bodies like the Institute of Psychoanalysis, represent a differing and separate strand within British psychiatry.

Sigmund and Anna Freud, International Psychoanalytical Congress, The Hague, 1920.

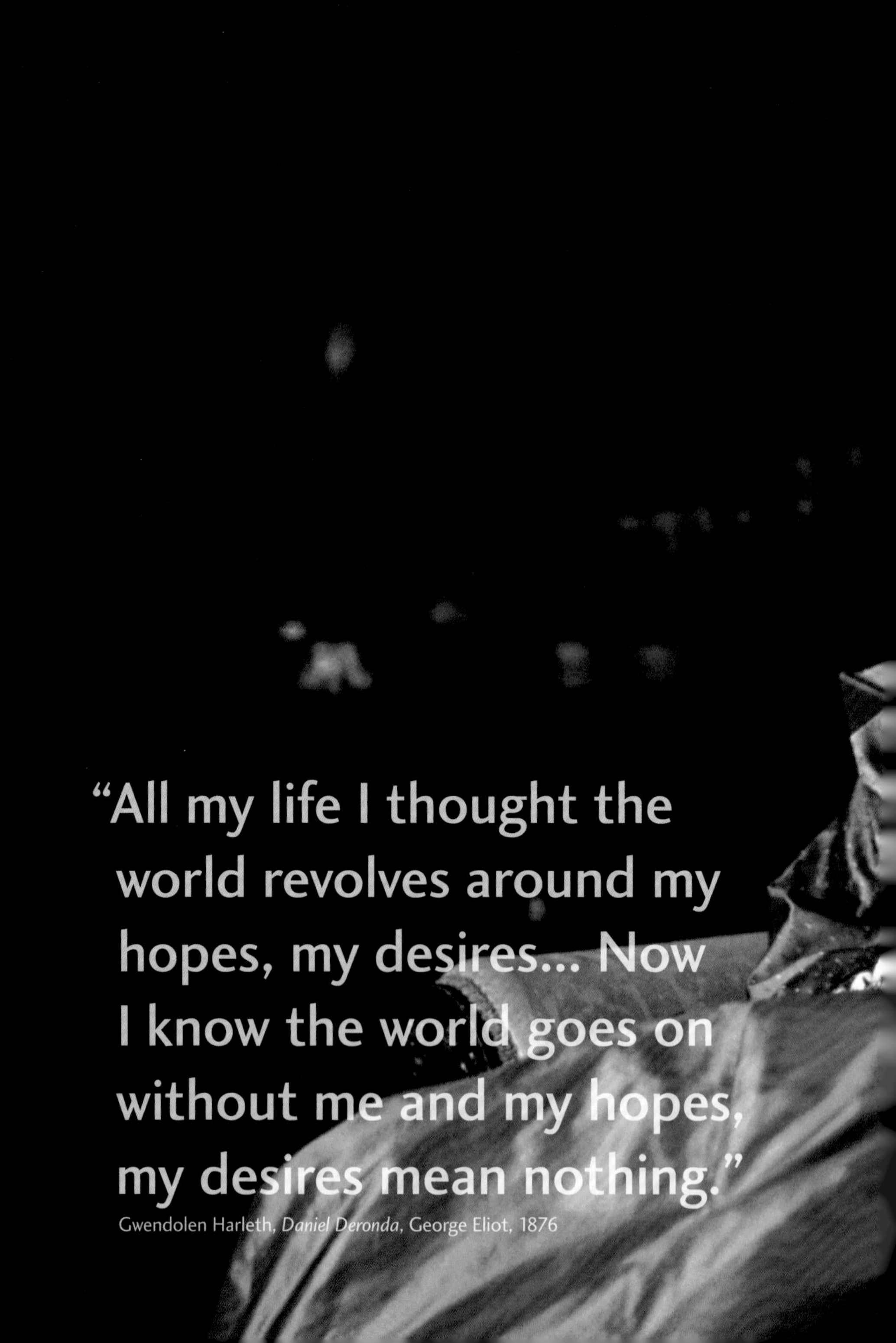

"All my life I thought the world revolves around my hopes, my desires... Now I know the world goes on without me and my hopes, my desires mean nothing."

Gwendolen Harleth, *Daniel Deronda*, George Eliot, 1876

Biographies D – F

George Eliot dedicated her novel *Daniel Deronda* to Emanuel Deutsch. It is one of the few novels written in that period that present Judaism and Jewish characters in a favourable light.

David Daube

Jurist

1909–1999

David Daube was born in Baden, Germany, to father Jakob, a wine merchant, and mother Selma, née Ascher. Both parents were Orthodox Jews. Daube was educated at Berthold Gymnasium and studied law at Freiburg University. There he came to the attention of German-Jewish jurist Otto Lenel, the founder of the modern study of Roman law. Although retired, Lenel tutored Daube personally and Daube attained a distinction for his doctorate in 1932. His thesis was based on Old Testament law so couldn't be published under the Nazis' ruling; Daube would have to wait 30 years to receive his degree. In 1933 Daube was compelled to leave Germany, settling in England. He gained a doctorate in Roman law at Cambridge in 1936 and taught at various colleges from 1938 to 1951. Daube's first book, *Studies in Biblical Law*, was published in 1947. In 1951 he became Professor of Jurisprudence at Aberdeen, having turned down a post at the Hebrew University of Jerusalem. His 1956 paper "Rabbinic Judaism" proved to be his most substantial, and in 1959 Daube wrote a well-regarded paper on Roman law, which became one of his lasting contributions to the field. Daube was Regius Professor of Civil Law at Oxford, 1955–70, and became the most noted of Roman lawyers. He was a fellow of the British and Bavarian academies and was awarded several honorary degrees. In the 1980s he settled in California.

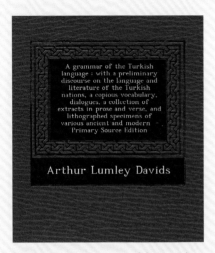

A grammar of the Turkish language : with a preliminary discourse on the language and literature of the Turkish nations, a copious vocabulary, dialogues, a collection of extracts in prose and verse, and lithographed specimens of various ancient and modern - . Primary Source Edition

Arthur Lumley Davids

Arthur Lumley Davids

Precocious linguist who fought for Jewish Emancipation

1811 – 1832

Arthur Lumley Davids was born in Hampshire. He was considered a child prodigy and showed a particular aptitude for mechanics, music and philosophy at school. His father died when he was just 10 years old. Davids moved with his mother to London, where he developed his passion for linguistics and began studying a remarkable number of languages including Turkish, Hebrew, Arabic and Persian as well as many European languages. He gave most of his attention to Turkish, and produced his *Grammar of the Turkish Language* in 1832. He dedicated his groundbreaking study to the Sultan of Turkey, Mahmud II. Davids' dreams of becoming a lawyer were crushed by antisemitic rules that prohibited him from being called to the bar. He consequently put his efforts behind the Jewish Emancipation movement and he frequently took to the *London Times* to argue for the cause. He helped found the Society for the Cultivation of Hebrew Literature, delivering a lecture at a meeting in 1830 on Jewish literature and philosophy. Davids died of cholera just weeks before his 21st birthday.

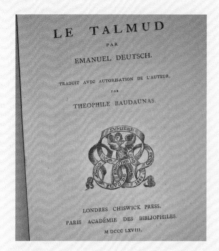

LE TALMUD

PAR

EMANUEL DEUTSCH.

TRADUIT AVEC AUTORISATION DE L'AUTEUR,

PAR

THEOPHILE BAUDAUNAS.

LONDRES CHISWICK PRESS.
PARIS ACADÉMIE DES BIBLIOPHILES.
M DCCC LXVIII.

Emanuel Oscar Menahem Deutsch

Talmudic scholar at the British Museum

1829–1873

Emanuel Deutsch was born into an observant family in Silesia, Prussia. His love for Middle Eastern culture began at home, where his uncle taught him about oriental languages and literature. After completing a degree in Talmudic studies and theology in Berlin, Deutsch left for England. On the recommendation of Asher Asher, he became an assistant in the library of the British Museum. While there, Deutsch wrote nearly 200 papers for *Chambers's Encyclopedia*, essays for biblical dictionaries and articles on the Bible and the Talmud. He also contributed to a work on Phoenician inscriptions published by the Museum's trustees. In 1867, Deutsch wrote an article for the *Quarterly Review* that brought him national recognition and sparked a wider interest in the Talmud. In the paper, he put forward the view that early Christianity owed much to pre-existing ideas found in the Talmud and wider ancient Palestinian writings. The essay was translated into six languages and was reprinted in English several times. Deutsch also worked for *The Times*, acting as Special Correspondent during the Vatican's Ecumenical Council of 1869. George Eliot dedicated her novel *Daniel Deronda* to Emanuel Deutsch as a thank you for the many Hebrew lessons he had given her. He died in Alexandria in 1873; a year later *Literary Remains*, a collection of 19 of his papers, was published.

Isaac Deutscher
Soviet exile in Britain
1907–1967

Isaac Deutscher was born in Galicia, Poland. He was part of an Orthodox, Hasidic sect and his father hoped he would become a rabbi. Deutscher however had abandoned his faith by the time of his barmitzvah. In his teens he started publishing poetry and went on to study literature, history and philosophy in Krakow but at 18 left for Warsaw, where he became a Marxist. In 1927 he joined the illegal Communist Party of Poland and in 1931 he travelled to Soviet Russia. He disliked the repression he saw under Stalin and, inspired by Leon Trotsky, became a leading figure in the Union of Communist Internationalists of Poland. He left for London to work as a correspondent for a Polish-Jewish newspaper in 1939. This move probably saved his life, as his family left behind in Poland were killed in Auschwitz. In Britain, he taught himself English and became a journalist for several respected publications including *The Economist* and the *Observer*. In the late 1940s he started publishing the works for which he is best known, including his biography of Stalin (1949) and his famous three-volume biography of Trotsky (1954–1963). These works displayed his eternal optimism and commitment to a socialist world, but they also set out the distinction between classical and vulgar/perverted Marxism. In the 1960s he became a popular figure with students in both the US and Britain and lectured at Cambridge, Princeton, Harvard and Columbia.

John Diamond
Fondly remembered journalist
1953–2001

John Diamond was born in Hackney into a secular Jewish household. His father was a biochemist and his mother a fashion designer. In 1992 he began to write for *The Sunday Times*. He got the job when his former boss, who wrote a regular column for the paper, went on holiday for three weeks and Diamond took over. The paper realised his talent and kept him on upon his boss's return. His weekly column "Something for the Weekend" explored a wide range of subjects including technology, cigars, cars and whisky. He met his wife Nigella Lawson at the paper and the pair married in Venice. After receiving a diagnosis of throat cancer, Diamond wrote *C: Because Cowards Get Cancer Too*, which was shortlisted for the Samuel Johnson Prize; it was adapted into a theatre play by Victoria Coren Mitchell. A second book, *Snake Oil and other Preoccupations*, was published posthumously. Diamond was not religious but began attending a synagogue near the end of his life so that his children could learn about their heritage. Diamond is remembered as ever-optimistic: he bought a new Harley-Davidson and got a tattoo upon his diagnosis and his final article for the *Observer* was entitled "Reasons to be Cheerful".

"Why am I happy? Because I'm alive… You aren't happy? Yes you are: this, here, now, is what happiness is. Enjoy it."

John Diamond, The Observer, December 2000

Isaac D'Israeli

His writing inspired
his statesman son
1766–1848

Isaac D'Israeli was born in
London to Italian merchant
Benjamin and his wife Sarah. His
father hoped that he would go
into business but from an early
age Isaac harboured aspirations
to be a writer. In 1791 he published the highly successful *Curiosities of Literature,* which ran to a total of six volumes. The work was a
compilation of biographical anecdotes, a style much in favour at
the time. He followed this with a number of novels and *The Literary
Character* (1818), a study of the geniuses of the day. In 1828,
D'Israeli wrote *Commentaries of the Life and Reign of Charles I,* which
was a sympathetic portrayal of the ill-fated monarch. It is believed
that the work influenced the Tory ideas of his son, the future prime
minister Benjamin Disraeli. Isaac was a member of the Bevis Marks
Synagogue, but after a disagreement with the elders he left the
congregation in 1821. He claimed that the synagogue's services were
"disturbing" and did not "excite religious emotions". Isaac had his
children baptised into the Christian faith as he believed this would
offer them more social success. However, Isaac himself did not leave
the Jewish faith and became associated with the new West London
Synagogue – the first Reform Synagogue in Britain – in Berkeley
Street, London.

Alfred Edersheim

From Yeshiva Student to
Christian Minister
1825–1889

Alfred Edersheim was born in
Vienna to banker Marcus and his
wife Stephanie (née Beifuss). He
was educated at a Hebrew school
and then the University of Vienna.
In the early 1840s Edersheim
travelled to Hungary, where he joined a local Presbyterian community.
He converted to Christianity and joined them on their return
journey to Scotland. After completing studies in Christian theology,
Edersheim became a Presbyterian minister. He travelled back across
the Channel and preached to Germans and Jews living in Romania.
Later, he established the first Presbyterian community in Devon. After
moving to the Church of England Edersheim became a preacher at the
University of Oxford, where he also lectured as a Grinfield lecturer on
the Greek translation of the Old Testament, the Septuagint. A prolific
writer, Edersheim translated many Christian philosophical works from
German to English. In 1883 he wrote his famous historical work, *The
Life and Times of Jesus the Messiah*. It is not clear why Edersheim
abandoned his Jewish roots but it appears he retained an interest
in Hebraic culture. His vast personal library, which contained a large
Hebrew collection, is now housed at Exeter College, Oxford.

Norbert Elias
Sought to understand the
Holocaust through sociology
1897–1990

Norbert Elias was born in
Breslau, Germany, now Wroclaw,
Poland. He fought in the First
World War for the German
army and afterwards studied
philosophy and medicine at
Breslau University. Elias fled Germany following Hitler's rise to power,
initially finding refuge in Paris and then settling in England. Elias
became a senior research fellow at the London School of Economics
in 1939 but was forced to postpone his work when he was interned
as an enemy alien. In the midst of this unsettled time, Elias was
writing his most important work, *The Civilizing Process* (1939), which
examined the west's assumed civilised superiority. Elias noted that
while this apparent superiority seemed inherent to Europeans, these
characteristics were the end result of a long civilising process. The
work was, in part, Elias's way of making sense of the atrocities that
had befallen the Jews during the war and, on a personal level, the loss
of his mother at Auschwitz. He became Emeritus Professor at the
University of Frankfurt in 1971 and was awarded the first Theodor W.
Adorno prize in 1977. Elias was a passionate Zionist in his youth and
was a member of the Blau-Weiss youth group, but later sought to
hide this fact.

Richard Ellmann

He outlined the development
of Irish literature

1918–1987

Richard Ellmann was born in
Detroit, Michigan to Romanian
lawyer James Ellmann and his
Ukrainian wife Jeanette. His
father had trained at the famous
Slobodka Yeshiva in Lithuania
and had come to the United States to lead a large Orthodox
community, yet Ellmann did not overtly identify with his Jewish
heritage. He studied at Yale University and after the war he travelled
to Trinity College, Dublin to undertake graduate work. Here he met
Georgia Hyde-Lees, the widow of the poet W. B. Yeats, who gave
Ellmann access to her personal archive; the result was the well-
received *Yeats: The Man and the Masks* (1949). Ellmann is best known
for his biography of James Joyce (1959), which earned him the title
of the most "outstanding literary biographer of his generation." He
won the US National Book Award for Nonfiction and published a
new edition in 1982 after consulting previously unseen sources. In
addition to his many essays on writers including Samuel Beckett, T.
S. Eliot and Ezra Pound he edited *The New Oxford Book of American
Verse* and was co-editor of two anthologies of modern poetry. Ellmann
held a number of academic positions, including the Goldsmiths Chair
of English Literature at Oxford. Shortly before his death and in spite
of his struggle with motor neurone disease, he finished a biography
of Oscar Wilde.

Geoffrey Elton

He introduced us to
Tudor politics
1921–1994

Geoffrey Elton, formerly
Gottfried Ehrenberg, the son of
a classical scholar, was born in
Tübingen, Germany. His family
were thoroughly assimilated
German Jews, so much so that
the death of his grandfather was marked by a wreath from Kaiser
Wilhelm II. The family moved to Prague in 1929 and to England in
1939. Geoffrey attended Rydal School in north Wales and took an
external University of London degree, from where he also gained a
doctorate. He began lecturing at Cambridge University in 1949 and
became the Regius Professor. He is best known for his contribution
to the history of Tudor England, with books such as *The Tudor
Revolution in Government*, which argued that Thomas Cromwell was the
creator of the modern bureaucratic government. While his Cromwell
thesis has been widely challenged, he made a significant contribution
to the discussion of the period. Through books such as *The Practice
of History* he also contributed to the debate on the philosophy
of historical practice. He believed in the value of political history
and the agency of the individual and opposed socio-economic
explanations of change. He became Fellow of the British Academy
in 1967 and President of the Royal Historical Society in 1972, and
was knighted in 1986. The writer and comedian Ben Elton is Geffrey
Elton's nephew.

Isidore Epstein
Rabbi and rabbinical scholar
1894–1962

Isidore Epstein was born in Kovno, Lithuania. He was educated at the Pressburg Yeshiva, then studied in Paris under the chief rabbi of France, Rabbi Zadoc Kahn. Epstein settled in Britain and after a short period as rabbi of Middleborough, he joined the staff of Jews' College in London in 1928. There he remained, rising to director of studies in 1945, and was subsequently appointed principal. He was an able administrator and inspiring leader, and as a teacher he could readily put his students in their place with his stock put-down: "you don't know your Bible!" Epstein was also a rabbinical scholar of some note. He was one of the editors of Joseph H. Hertz' *Pentateuch and Haftorahs* (1929–1936). The work was published in 1935, as part of the celebration of the eighth centenary of the birth of Maimonides. Epstein's greatest achievement was as the editor of the first complete English translation of the Babylonian Talmud for the Soncino Press. For this mammoth task, comprising 36 volumes written between 1935 and 1952, Epstein recruited the assistance of numerous scholars and rabbis. However, he kept a close eye on every detail of the project, personally reviewing and annotating each element as it was written.

Samuel Jacob Hayyim Falk

"Baal-Shem" and alchemist
c.1710–1782

Samuel Jacob Hayyim Falk was born in Galicia. He spent some time in Furth, in modern northern Bavaria, before moving to Westphalia. There his alchemical practices led to his being accused of witchcraft and sentenced to death. He escaped and settled in London in 1742. Falk made his home in Wellclose Square, where he also established a private synagogue. More public, though, were his occult activities; he opened a magical-alchemical laboratory on London Bridge, attracting interest and attention from Jews and non-Jews alike. The diaries of Hirsch Kalish, Falk's personal assistant for the years 1747–51, detailed his bizarre life and his clashes with London's Jewish community. But if Falk upset the Jewish community, he was a legendary figure for Christian freemasons and occultists. He counted among those fascinated by his glamour such high-society fans as a Corsican king, a Polish prince, the Duke of Orleans and the Marquis de la Croix. Falk also promoted a new version of Judeo-Christian freemasonry based around the Cabbala. Falk was a mixture of the spiritual and the intensely practical, sometimes successful in extorting large sums of money from his supporters. He was the subject of a notorious painting, wrongly attributed to John Singleton Copley, which showed him in eastern robes with mystical paraphernalia. Due to this portrayal Falk was believed for some time to be the Baal Shem Tov, the founder of the Hasidic movement in eastern Europe. Thus Falk was a master of illusion even after death.

Philip Ferdinand

A prolific scholar of rabbinic
literature in Tudor England
1556–1599

Philip Ferdinand was born in
Poland and received a traditional
Talmudic education in addition
to his general schooling. In the
1580s he travelled throughout
the Middle East. Around 1585 he
converted to Roman Catholicism, but sometime later moved to the
Church of England. In 1595 Ferdinand moved to England, where he
tutored in Hebrew at the Universities of both Oxford and Cambridge.
Ferdinand is best known for his translation and interpretation of
different rabbinic works and introducing them to new audiences
in England. His most famous book, entitled *Haec Sunt Verba Dei*,
contains an interpretation of the 613 commandments found in
the Torah. His commentaries were widely used at the time by both
students and professors of Semitic culture. In 1599 he moved to
Holland, where he became a successful tutor in Hebrew and Arabic
at the University of Leiden. Before his death later that year, he
introduced the student body and his colleagues to many aspects of
Jewish literature and culture.

Eva Figes

Feminist and writer

1932–2012

Eva Unger was born in Berlin. Her parents were Emil Edward Unger, a company director, and his wife Irma Alice née Cohen. On Kristallnacht in 1938, Emil was arrested and transported to Dachau concentration camp. After his release he escaped to England with his family, arriving in March 1939. Eva was educated at Kingsbury Grammar School and graduated from Queen Mary College at the University of London with a BA in English. She was determined to become a writer. She married George Figes in 1954 but the couple divorced in 1962. Figes published her first book, *Equinox*, in 1966. Her second novel, *Winter Journey*, won the Guardian prize for fiction. In 1970 *Patriarchal Attitudes*, an examination of women's place in society, garnered much press attention. She later said that she counted herself "lucky to have written the right book at the right moment." Figes experimented with the structure of the modern novel. One work, *Waking* (1981), followed a woman's experience of waking from a seven-day sleep; another, *Light* (1983), was based on one day in the life of Claude Monet. Figes remained in London for the rest of her life, but retained the vestiges of a German accent. She took a critical stance on Israel, and in one of her final works, *Journey to Nowhere* (2008), she explored a young German woman's disappointment upon reaching the Promised Land.

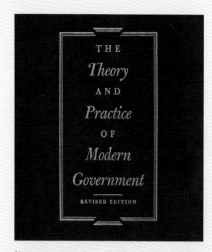

THE
Theory
AND
Practice
OF
Modern
Government
REVISED EDITION

Herman Finer
Political scientist
1898–1969

Herman Finer was born in Hertsa, in the former kingdom of Romania. His parents were Max Finer and his wife Fanny, née Weiner. Max and Fanny immigrated to Britain from Romania. Initially making a living as market traders, they later opened their own drapery shop. Herman became associated with the Fabian Society, a British socialist organisation that pledged to further the principles of democratic socialism through gradualist and reformist efforts, rather than revolutionary overthrow. He took a keen interest in the mechanisms and theories of government, both at home and abroad. His major works included *Foreign Governments at Work* (1921), *The Theory and Practice of Modern Government* (1932) and *English Local Government* (1933). Finer taught for many years at the University of Chicago, and remained in the city until his death.

Samuel Finer

Political Scientist

1915–1993

Samuel Finer was born in Islington, London to immigrant Romanian parents. He was educated at Holloway Grammar School and Trinity College, Oxford. His academic career began at Balliol College, Oxford and from there he went on to build up politics departments at both Keele and Manchester Universities before returning to Oxford. His classic text *Comparative Government* has been reprinted many times. He was a prolific writer and produced the first complete study of British pressure groups in *Anonymous Empire*; In *The Man on Horseback* he examined the role of the military in politics and as Gladstone Professor of Government and Public Administration at All Souls College, Oxford, he produced important studies of the British party and electoral systems. He was elected a fellow of the British Academy in 1982. He brought up his children with an understanding of their Jewish religion and heritage and he himself maintained some religious observances. He was President of the Jewish Students' Society at Manchester University and defended Israel in university debates. His most ambitious book, *The History of Government from the Earliest Times*, was published posthumously. Fishman was heavily involved in the genesis and development of the Jewish Museum London.

Moses Finley

Historian, classical scholar
and sociologist
1912–1986

Moses Finley, né Finkelstein, was
born in New York and studied
at Syracuse University where
he read psychology, followed
by a master's degree in public
law at Columbia University.
He subsequently held research posts at Columbia and Rutgers
Universities. In 1954 he moved to England following investigations
by the McCarran Security Committee during the communist witch-
hunt. He started lecturing at Cambridge and became a professor
of ancient history. He was a prolific writer of books, articles and
chapters and was highly regarded, especially in France and Italy. In
1975 he was described in the *New York Review of Books* as "the most
influential ancient historian of our time." He was interested in the
sociology of the ancient world and his books were scholarly yet also
accessible to the general reader. His best-known works include *The
Ancient Economy, Ancient Slavery and Modern Ideology* and *The World
of Odysseus*. He became a fellow of the British Academy in 1971, was
welcomed back to the USA in 1972 as a visiting lecturer and was
knighted in 1979.

William J. Fishman
Radical historian and educator
who inspired many
1921–2014

William J. Fishman was born in
the East End of London in 1921
to an immigrant tailoring family.
He left school at the age of 14,
working initially as a clerk. The
following year he joined the
Labour League of Youth and witnessed the Battle of Cable Street. His
experiences of seeing Jews and Irish dock workers uniting to stand
up to fascism sparked off a lifelong commitment to education and
uncovering the histories of working people. Fishman's early career
as a teacher was interrupted by Second World War service in the Far
East. During the mid-1950s he combined teaching with studying
for a degree at the London School of Economics, followed by a
fellowship at Balliol College, Oxford. He held appointments at several
US universities, before being appointed Barnet Shine Senior Research
Fellow in Labour Studies at Queen Mary, University of London. 1974
saw the publication of *East End Jewish Radicals 1875–1914*, which
illuminated the lives of a community of Jewish anarchists, showing
them as agents of change. This was followed in 1988 by *East End
1888: Life in a London Borough Among the Labouring Poor*, which took
a wider look at the area's working-class population. When he died at
the age of 93 he was remembered for his powerful and vivid tours of
the East End, which were an inspiration to a new generation of East
End historians and tour guides. Fishman was heavily involved in the
genesis and development of the Jewish Museum London.

Meyer Fortes

Enhanced our understanding of
kinship and family structure
1906–1983

Meyer Fortes was born in
Britstown, Cape Colony. His
grandfather had escaped
conscription in the Russian
army by moving to England
and his father in turn had left
England for South Africa. Fortes read English and psychology at
the University of Cape Town and his impressive work there earned
him a place at University College London, where he undertook his
PhD in psychology. The shift in his work to anthropology came after
he met Bronislaw Malinowski and joined his seminar at the London
School of Economics. During the 1930s, Fortes conducted extensive
research abroad, including a three-year research project in Ghana.
The result of this extensive study of tribal relationships includes
his 1945 book, *The Dynamics of Clanship among the Tallensi*. Fortes
began a readership in anthropology at the LSE in 1946 before taking
the William Wyse chair at Cambridge in 1950. He stayed in touch
with his Jewish roots and joined the Jewish Child Guidance Centre in
1930 as a clinical psychologist and later became the president of the
Cambridge Friends of the Hebrew University.

Eduard Fraenkel

One of the foremost classical
scholars of his time
1888–1970

Eduard David Mortier Fraenkel
was born in Berlin, the son
of Julius Fraenkel and Edith
Heimann, both of Jewish descent.
He attended the Askanisches
Gymnasium and then studied
law at the University of Berlin, before transferring to Göttingen to
study his true passion: classical philology. He moved to Berlin in
1917 and was appointed Privatdozent; he became a full professor
at Kiel in 1923. After Hitler's rise to power in 1933, Fraenkel, owing
to his Jewish status, was forbidden from teaching and so moved to
Oxford. There he was elected to the Corpus Chair of Latin at Oxford
in 1934, a post that he held until his retirement. He was naturalised
as a British citizen in 1939. Fraenkel published several important
works including a book on Horace in 1957, one on Aristophanes in
1962 and an important study of Latin word order and prose rhythm
in 1968. He was a fellow of the British Academy from 1941 to 1964,
and the recipient of the Kenyon Medal in 1965. He was awarded
honorary degrees from the Universities of West Berlin, Urbino,
St Andrews, Florence, Fribourg and Oxford.

ENCYCLOPEDIA
TALMUDICA

A DIGEST OF HALACHIC LITERATURE AND JEWISH LAW
FROM THE TANNAITIC PERIOD TO THE PRESENT TIME
ALPHABETICALLY ARRANGED

Founder and Editor
THE LATE RABBI MEYER BERLIN (BAR-ILAN)
Editor
RABBI SHLOMO JOSEF ZEVIN
Director
RABBI JEHOSHUA HUTNER

English Translation Edited by
THE LATE PROF. ISIDORE EPSTEIN (LONDON)
And
RABBI DR. HARRY FREEDMAN (AUSTRALIA)

VOLUME I
אלף

"YAD HARAV HERZOG" – RABBI HERZOG WORLD ACADEMY

Harry Freedman
Rabbi and translator
1901–1982

Harry Mordecai Freedman was born in Vitebsk, Russia. His family emigrated to Britain and he was raised in London. He was educated at the Etz Chaim Yeshiva, an Ashkenazi Orthodox yeshiva in Golders Green. He went on to the University of London, as a *semicha* from Jews' College, a qualification whereby a Jewish man can become a rabbi. He was later awarded a PhD, also from the University of London. Freedman made significant contributions to the translation of Jewish sacred texts, and his major works included eight volumes of the *Babylonian Talmud* as part of the Soncino English edition of the Talmud, and the *Encyclopedia Talmudica*, the English edition of *Encyclopedia Talmudit*. He also translated several volumes of Menachem Mendel Kasher's *Torah Sheleimah*, known in English as *The Encyclopedia of Biblical Interpretation*. Freedman served in pulpit positions in England, the United States and Australia, and taught at Yeshiva University in New York.

Anna Freud

Led the field of child
psychoanalysis
1895–1982

Anna Freud was born in Vienna,
the youngest daughter of
Sigmund and Martha Freud.
She was raised as a secular
Jew, and educated at the Salka
Goldman Cottage Lyceum.
After working as an elementary school teacher, she followed in her
father's footsteps and became interested in child psychoanalysis.
As chairman of the Vienna Psychoanalytic Society, Freud published
a paper in 1927 outlining her approach to child psychoanalysis,
and gave lectures on her findings to parents and teachers. When
the Nazis entered Vienna in 1938, the family moved to Hampstead,
London. After the Second World War, Freud founded the
Hampstead Child Therapy Clinic, serving as its director until 1982.
From the 1950s onwards, she travelled regularly to the United
States to lecture, and was elected as a Foreign Honorary Member
of the American Academy of Arts and Sciences in 1959. Freud's
most important and influential work on child psychology, *Normality
and Pathology in Childhood,* was published in 1968. She was awarded
a CBE in 1967 and numerous honorary doctorates and fellowships.
Following her death, the Hampstead Child Therapy Clinic she
founded was renamed the Anna Freud Centre. She was a keen
equestrian and loved to read detective novels.

Sigmund Freud
The father of psychoanalysis
1856–1939

Sigismund Freud, who abbreviated his name to Sigmund at 22, was born in Pribor, Moravia, now part of the Czech Republic. Though Judaism was culturally a big part of Freud's identity, he himself was an atheist. The family settled in Vienna when Freud was a boy, and in 1873 he began his medical studies at Vienna University. After receiving his medical qualification in 1881, Freud began a residency at the Viennese General Hospital and collaborated with Josef Breuer in treating hysteria by means of hypnosis. He set up his private practice in 1886, specialising in nervous and brain disorders. Freud is best known for developing the psychoanalytic theory of the conscious mind (the ego), the unconscious (the id) and the conscience (superego). His magnum opus, *The Interpretation of Dreams*, published in 1900, spoke about dreams in terms of unconscious desires. Other influential works include *The Psychopathology of Everyday Life* (1901) and *The Ego and the Id*, published in 1923. Freud was appointed Professor of Neuropathology at the University of Vienna in 1902, a post he held until 1938, when he was forced to flee Nazi-occupied Austria and settled in Hampstead, London. Freud, who was a cigar smoker all his life, died from jaw cancer. His impact continues to be felt in academia and popular culture.

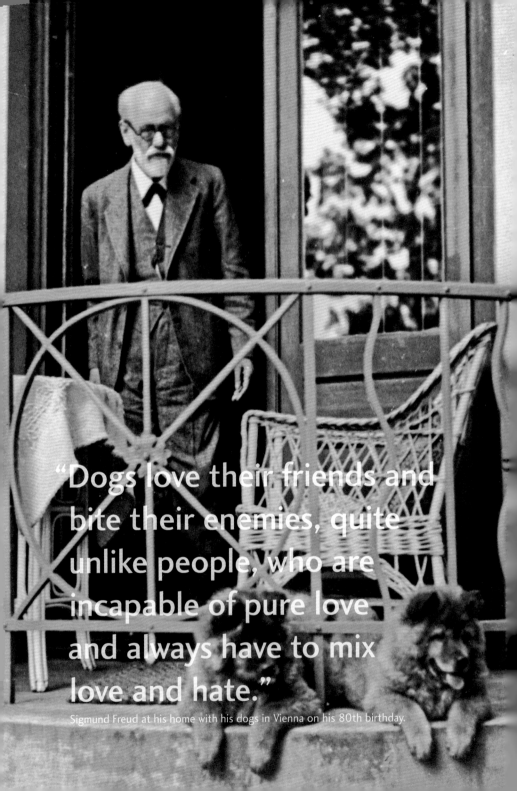

"Dogs love their friends and bite their enemies, quite unlike people, who are incapable of pure love and always have to mix love and hate."

Sigmund Freud at his home with his dogs in Vienna on his 80th birthday.

Michael Friedländer

Orientalist and Principal
of Jews' College
1833–1910

Michael Friedländer was born
in Jutroschin, Germany, in the
then Grand Duchy of Posen.
He was educated at a Catholic
school, but also attended cheder.
He attended the gymnasium,
continuing his Jewish studies under rabbis Joseph Oettinger and
Elchanan Rosenstein. He went on to read Classics and mathematics
at the Universities of Berlin and Halle. He settled in Berlin as principal
of the Talmud school there, before resigning in 1865 to accept the
role of principal of Jews' College London, where was appointed as
successor to Barnett Abrahams. At Jews' College he taught theology,
history, mathematics and Arabic. As a member of the Society of
Hebrew Literature he published many works under its imprint. They
included, most famously, a translation from the original Arabic of
Maimonides' *Guide of the Perplexed*. Friedländer retired from his
position in 1907. His son-in-law Moses Gaster continued his legacy
as leader of the Sephardi congregation in London and was a noted
Hebrew linguist.

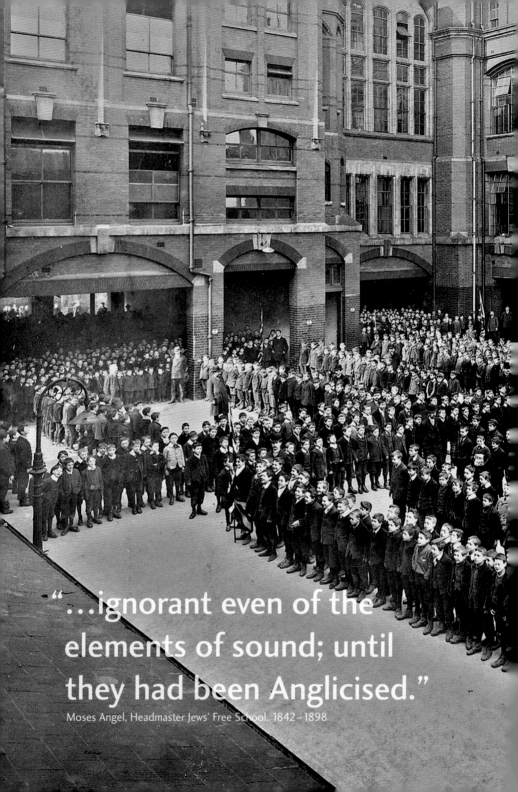

"...ignorant even of the elements of sound; until they had been Anglicised."

Moses Angel, Headmaster Jews' Free School. 1842–1898

Learning to be English...

In the 1880s and 1890s, the mass exodus of Jews from Eastern Europe meant that more than a third of the Jews' Free School pupils had been born abroad and, of those born in England, most were the children of recently arrived immigrants.

Jews' Free School, Middlesex Street, Petticoat Lane in the East End of London c.1900.

Learning to be English: the influence of the Jews' Free School

David Harris

Deputy Headteacher, Jews' Free School, 1986–2015

Before taking up my post at JFS, I spent a fascinating evening in the company of Nathan Rubin, the honorary correspondent of the governing body. Nat, one of the most influential figures in the history of the School, was a larger-than-life character. He had been recruited by Chief Rabbi Brodie from the London County Council and not only did he have an encyclopaedic knowledge of the minutiae of education legislation, but he would have you believe that he built the Camden school himself, brick by brick, and that wasn't far from the truth. Nat had invited me to his home for coffee and we spent the evening talking about the history and development of the School. It was during that conversation that I first heard a saying about the school that has since achieved cliché status in certain areas of the Anglo-Jewish community:

"You know, David," Nat said, "in the late 19th and early 20th centuries they used to say that the task of the Jews' Free School was to make Englishmen out of Jews [pause] and now the job of the JFS is to make Jews out of Englishmen!"

Now, clichés may be "expressions showing a lack of original thought" (*OED*), but they are also true. So, is this nothing more than a rather cute observation? Does it have anything serious to say? Well, let's see.

By 1900, the Jews' Free School, founded in 1732, was in full swing with an estimated 4,000 students on its Bell Lane site in Spitalfields.

Around half of the students had been born abroad, mainly in central and eastern Europe, while a similar number, although born in England, had parents who had arrived from overseas. Only 10 per cent of the student body had been born in England to English-born parents. This was a school overwhelmingly of immigrants; Jews who, escaping persecution in their homeland, had settled in London's East End but who seemed to have little in common with their brethren whose families had come to England after the readmission in 1656. Those Jews had done very well for themselves and had become accepted in their new home, even achieving entrées to the great and the good. The last thing they wanted was a horde of, in their perception, rough-looking, noisy, curiously attired, religious fanatics spoiling it for them.

Responding to the great wave of immigration of the 1880s, an editorial in the *Jewish Chronicle* (August 1881) proclaimed that "the foreign poor form a community within the community. They come mostly from Poland; they… bring Poland with them and they retain Poland while they stop here. This is most undesirable… Our outside world is not capable of making minute discrimination between Jew and Jew and forms its opinions of Jews in general as much, if not more, from them than from the anglicised portion of the community."

What was needed was a process of making these people English. "Anglicisation", it would be called, and the main vehicle would be the schools. As Israel Zangwill, pupil, pupil-teacher and teacher of the Jews' Free School, wrote in his 1892 masterpiece *Children of the Ghetto*, "the bell of the great Ghetto school [i.e. the Jews' Free] summoning its pupils from the reeking courts and alleys, from the garrets and the cellars, calling them to come and be anglicised."

But how do you do it? Well, the first step was an attack on Yiddish. Yiddish, originally a German dialect with words from Hebrew and other modern languages, was the *lingua franca* of Jewish central and eastern Europe. For the American writer Leo Rosten Yiddish was "a language of exceptional charm" even if it did "steal from the linguistically rich to give to the fledgling poor", and the journalist, Charles Rappaport, joked that "I speak ten languages – all of them in Yiddish."

But, for the men who governed the Jews' Free School, Yiddish had no charm; neither was it a subject for humour. It had come from the shtetls of Europe and that's where it should stay. Moses Angel, the inspirational and dynamic head teacher who led the School for over 50 years in the 19th century, thought Yiddish "an unintelligible language" that erected a barrier between the immigrant and the host country. Angel's successor, Louis Abrahams, agreed. For him it was "a miserable jargon which is not a language at all."

Further, Sir Samuel Montagu, later to become Lord Swaythling, advised the pupils to refuse to learn Yiddish from their parents. Indeed, he said, they should teach their parents to speak English. And so, except for a very short time when a new pupil started at the School, there would be no teaching in Yiddish at the Jews' Free. English was the language of the school and that was that.

But Yiddish wasn't the only barrier to anglicisation. Though immigrant parents were prepared to entrust their children to the schools for their secular studies, a majority was dissatisfied with the quantity and quality of religious education provided. They wanted a more intensive religious and Hebrew education than the School was able to provide. This vacuum was filled by the chedorim that sprouted everywhere in the East End. The children went to them after school and spent many a long hour there. Nonetheless, they remained popular with the parents – if not with the young people.

For the Jews' Free, however, chedorim and anglicisation were two opposites that most certainly could not attract and in December

Jew's Free School, photograph of a class during their first term at the school, 1908.

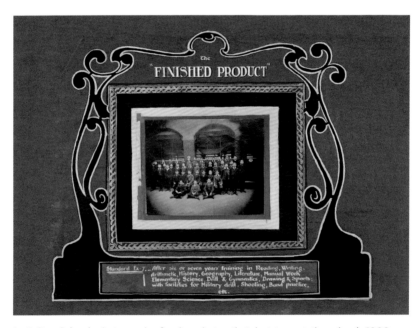

Jew's Free School, photograph of a class during their last term at the school, 1908.

1898, Lord Rothschild wrote to the parents of the boys on this very matter. The Rothschild family, much to the good fortune of the School, had chosen the Jews' Free as its favourite charity and that link remains to this day. But in those days "Rothschild…. was a magic name in the Ghetto; it stood next to the Almighty's as a redresser of grievances and a friend of the poor" (*Children of the Ghetto*).

Lord Rothschild saw his responsibilities to the families of the Jews' Free as extending beyond the mere handing over of cash. He knew what was best and parents would be doing their sons no good at all by insisting that they attend so many hours at cheder. Indeed, wrote His Lordship, the School's religious and Hebrew syllabus, issued and sanctioned by the Chief Rabbi, was perfectly adequate. Too much effort expended on Jewish studies would, without doubt, affect the boys' progress in secular studies and instead of getting on in the world, "they sink into the nick of ill-paid and over-crowded occupations and remain the mere drudges of society."

For Rothschild, chedorim stood in the way of the main purpose of the Jews' Free, which, after all, was to ensure that its pupils "grow up…. fitted in every way to pursue an honourable career, and with a reasonable prospect of becoming good and worthy English citizens."

The Jews' Free was, then, the enemy of the chedorim and, together with the Jewish Religious Education Board, tried to replace them by having its own teachers teach religious education in school after hours. Even so, and despite Lord Rothschild's sermon, as late as 1937 there were still nine of them between Mile End station and Shoreditch station and it was only really the dispersal of the East End community during the Second World War that led to their demise.

Also, the pupils' parents' east European lifestyles were frowned upon. They were urged to "throw off their foreign habits and foreign prejudices and become English – truly English." Everything that the

School attempted to do would be wasted if the children left their English school and returned to a Russian or Polish home.

Zangwill, of course, knew all about anglicisation. In his story *The Red Mark*, he tells of Bloomah Beckenstein, who knows that if everyone in her class attends school for a complete week, the class will be awarded the Banner. But Bloomah can't attend regularly. Her mother needs her at home. One day, however, Bloomah manages to evade her mother and go to school. But Mrs Beckenstein isn't having any of that and marches into school to drag Bloomah home to attend to her domestic duties. Now, that might be acceptable in Ukraine, but not in England, and Louis Abrahams was quick to point out to parents that "home training must supplement and support the School's training".

Nonetheless, and despite Mrs Beckenstein, anglicisation was a success. Empire Day, first introduced in 1904, was celebrated with considerable fervour and more than 1,200 former pupils fought in the First World War and suffered their proportionate share of death and injury. The head at the time, Laurence (né Lazar) Bowman, a Polish-born orphan and former pupil, wrote in the school magazine of July 1915 that it was wonderful to see "such unity of purpose with all other Britons in this hour of destiny". Sadly, in August 1917 Bowman's own son was killed in action in Flanders.

Moreover, anglicisation did not end with The Great War. A former pupil, Doron Zur, wrote many years later: "I arrived at JFS Camden Town in April of 1969 from the State of Israel… I came from a country with a completely different mentality, very much estranged from the British mentality. I came from a country which applied different behavioural codes in both manners and conduct. I shall ever be indebted to my British educators who have made me into a mature, well-educated true British gentleman."

So, the battle had been fought and won. The graduates of the
Jews' Free went on to build lives, families and futures as fully paid-
up Englishmen and they would contribute to all areas of life, both
Jewish and elsewhere. Joe Loss, Alfred Marks and Bud Flanagan
would become household names in the world of light entertainment.
Barney Barnato, who founded the De Beer diamond empire, was
a Jews' Free boy; so was Samuel Gompers, the first president of
the American Federation of Labour. And this tradition would be
continued beyond Bell Lane by, among others, Labour Party guru
Maurice (later Lord) Glassman, Barbara Roche MP, the actor Gina
Bellman, broadcaster and journalist Charles Golding and one of
my students, Dean Furman, currently the captain of South Africa's
football team.

The site in Bell Lane that had given so much to so many was
evacuated at the outbreak of war in 1939 and subsequently
destroyed by the Luftwaffe in 1941. But its pupils were a success
story. In fact, given their starting point, nothing short of a miracle.
They would leave the East End and set up home in one or other of
London's leafy suburbs in an environment very different from the
chaos and noise of where they had been brought up.

After a drawn-out and frequently acrimonious debate, the school
reopened in 1958 in Camden Town, admitting a totally different
generation of Jews. These young people were not immigrants; they
had not been brought up in poverty and their only language was
English. Their parents wanted better for them than they had had. A
profession, a mortgage, university. These young people were English
all right but how Jewish were they? How did the School address the
second part of the cliché and seek to make Jews out of Englishmen?

Well, therein lies a tale and to have been involved in this
development was truly exciting. With creativity and vision, the Jews'

Free School – now officially named JFS because Jo Wagerman, head teacher from 1985 to 1990, felt that "Jews' Free School sounds like something out of Dickens" – met the challenge of creating generations of young Jews who would be proud, committed and knowledgeable, aware of who they are and where they come from. But this is a tale for another time, although here's an anecdote by way of illustration:

A 14-year-old JFS girl of my acquaintance – let's call her Deborah – is travelling to a shiva with her parents. On the way, they are discussing Jewish mourning practices and laws. At some stage in this conversation, Deborah's father says to her: "How come you know so much about all of this?"

"That's a silly question, isn't it?" replied Deborah, "I go to a Jewish school, don't I?"

Opposite Jew's Free School,the only remaining building after the bombing of 1941.

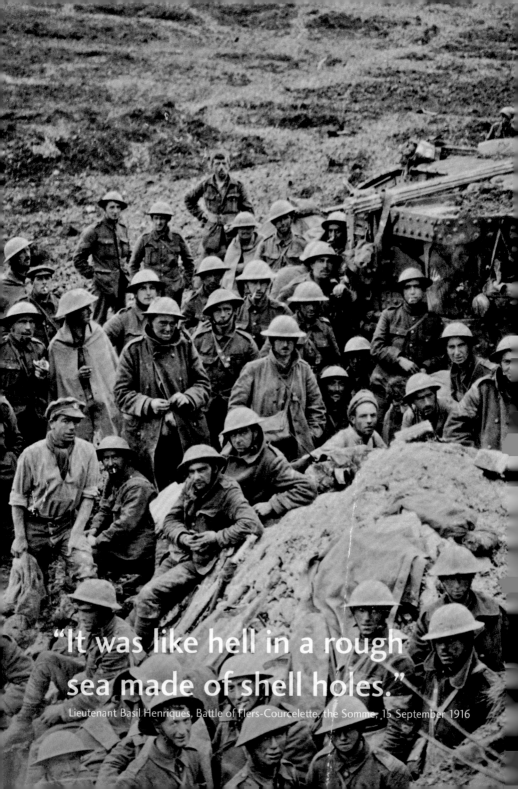

"It was like hell in a rough sea made of shell holes."

Lieutenant Basil Henriques, Battle of Flers-Courcelette, the Somme, 15 September 1916

Biographies G – H

Tanks were used in battle for the first time
in history at the Battle of Flers-Courcelette,
15–22 September 1916. Called Mark 1, the
first tanks were were crewed by an officer,
such as Basil Henriques, three drivers and
four gunners in appalling internal conditions
of extreme heat, noise and exhaust fumes.

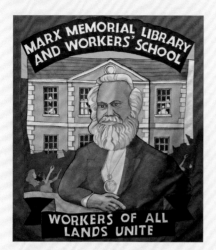

Jack Gaster
Lawyer and revolutionary
1907–2007

Jack Gaster was born in Maida Vale, London, the 12th of 13 children. His father was Dr Moses Gaster and his mother was Lucy Friedländer. Moses was expelled from Romania in 1885, and became Chief Rabbi of the Sephardi community in Britain. He was educated at the London School of Economics before embarking on a career in the law. He became an articled clerk in 1925, qualified in 1931 and in 1932 founded a law firm with partner Richard Turner. As his legal career proceeded, Gaster pursued a parallel interest in radical politics. In 1926, following the turmoil of the General Strike, he joined the Independent Labour Party, and became a passionate advocate for workers' rights. His house became a hub for dissenters, and in 1935 he left the ILP for the more radical Communist Party. After suffering a smashed elbow that kept him out of combat during the Second World War, he was elected onto the London County Council in company with only two other communists. He found a political home in the 1980s in Arthur Scargill's Socialist Labour Party, and was deeply critical of New Labour. Campaigning until the end, in his later years he poured his reforming energies into the pensioner movement and the Marx Memorial Library.

Moses Gaster
Scholar and rabbi
1856–1939

Moses Gaster was born in
Bucharest, Romania. His parents
were Abraham Emanuel Gaster
and Phina Judith Rubinstein.
Gaster went to the Universities
of Bucharest and Leipzig. On
graduation he attended the
rabbinical seminary at Breslau. He was ordained in 1881, and in that
year he returned to Bucharest to lecture in comparative mythology
and Romanian literature. Through his activities on behalf of other
Romanian Jews, he drew the gaze of the authorities, and was expelled
from Romania in 1855. He found safe haven in England, where in
1890 he married Leah Lucy, only daughter of Michael Friedländer. In
1886 he was invited to become Ilchester Lecturer at the University
of Oxford, an honour he was awarded once more in 1891. He was
the first to translate the Jewish liturgy into Romanian (1883). In
1887 Gaster was appointed haham or "wise man" of the Spanish and
Portuguese Jews in England – in effect, their chief rabbi. In the face
of fierce opposition from the leadership of the Sephardi community,
Gaster became a passionate supporter of political Zionism, and
took great pride in his part in the triumph of the movement. In 1929
he became an honorary member of the Romanian Academy, and in
1930 was elected a fellow of the Royal Society for Literature. Gaster
is remembered as one of the most accomplished linguists of his age.
The Gaster Papers – now housed at University College London – are
in ten languages.

Theodor Gaster
Scholar of myth and religion
1906–1992

Theodor Hertzl Gaster was born in London. He was the 13th son of Moses Gaster, Chief Rabbi of London. He was named after Theodor Hertzl, founder of Zionism and great friend to Moses. Theodor recalled that the first draft of the Balfour Declaration was prepared in his father's home, and that visitors to the house included Churchill, Lenin and Freud. Much of his early education came from reading aloud to his father once Moses' sight had failed. Gaster then read Greek, Latin and archaeology at the University of London. In 1943 he received his PhD from Columbia University in the United States. From 1968 to 1972 he was chairman of the religion department at Barnard College, teaching there and at Columbia University in an academic career that spanned five decades. His great work was as one of the original team of translators of the Dead Sea Scrolls, which were discovered in the late 1940s. His book *Dead Sea Scriptures* sold over 200 000 copies. He was known to his colleagues as an "Old-Fashioned Scholar", as archaic as his subjects. "That world is gone," he used to say. He was well known for rasping "Go away!" to any timid student who dared knock at his door. But he was much admired for his scholarship, known to be literate in 29 dialects and languages.

Ernest Gellner

Continually crossed
cultural boundaries
1925–1995

Ernest Gellner was a
social anthropologist and
philosopher. He was born in
Paris to Czech parents Rudolf
and Anna. Ernest came to
England at the age of 17 after
the Nazi takeover of Czechoslovakia. After studying at Oxford, he
was appointed lecturer in philosophy at the University of Edinburgh
and then to a position at the London School of Economics. In 1959
Gellner published a scathing attack on the work of Oxford linguistic
philosophers. This prompted a month-long heated exchange in *The
Times*. His other great contribution was to the study of nationalism.
Gellner proposed that in the modern, industrial world, national
powers needed to encourage a common culture and nationalist
sentiment in order to maintain authority. Gellner wrote about many
other subjects including the Soviet Union and Islamic societies.
He was known for his generosity, always making time for colleagues
and students despite his battle with bone disease. His uncle was
Julius Gellner, one of the most famous European theatre directors
of the early 20th century.

Norman Geras

Unorthodox Marxist thinker
1943–2013

Norman Geras was born into a Jewish family in Bulawayo, Southern Rhodesia. He moved to the UK in 1962 to read philosophy, politics and economics at Pembroke College, Oxford. In 1965 he moved to Nuffield College, Oxford as a research student, and in 1967 took up a lecturing role at the University of Manchester, where he gave a weekly seminar on Marxism. Indeed it was this topic that was the concern of his best-known work, including an exploration of Rosa Luxemburg's revolutionary politics. Geras began editing the *New Left Review* in 1976 and the *Socialist Register* in 1995; his ideas, however, were often anathema to the Orthodox left and he eventually established an online channel through which he could present his unfiltered opinions: *normblog*. There he made his case for the Iraq invasion, arguing that the west had an obligation to prevent further misery under Saddam Hussein's regime.

Martin Gilbert

Scholar and historian

1936–2015

Martin Gilbert was born in London. His grandparents came to Britain as refugees from Tsarist Russia. During the Second World War he was evacuated to Canada and then to Wales. On returning to London he was educated at Highgate School and Magdalen College, Oxford. He remained in Oxford to become a research scholar at St Antony's College and then a fellow at Merton College. He was a prolific writer, producing 88 books in his lifetime, in addition to being Churchill's official biographer. He wrote extensively on the Holocaust and often drew upon survivor testimony for his research. His works also covered the two World Wars, the return of the Jews to Israel and the struggles of Jews in Arab lands. He received a CBE in 1990 and a knighthood in 1995 for services to British history and international relations. In 2005 he was invited to serve as a member of the Chilcot Inquiry into the Iraq war. Martin Gilbert was a committed Zionist and a proudly observant Jew, regularly attending Highgate Synagogue. His books of Jewish maps remain an important resource for historians to this day.

Morris Ginsberg

Sociologist who studied the
structure of Jewish life
1889–1970

Morris Ginsberg was born in
Kelmy, Lithuania. He was given
a traditional Jewish education
in his small religious community
and arrived in England in
1904 to work at his father's
tobacco factory knowing only the Yiddish language. But Ginsberg
was determined to take further education and was rewarded for his
tireless efforts with a sociology scholarship to study at University
College London. He graduated with a first-class degree in philosophy
and sociology and was invited by his supervisor Leonard Hobhouse
to assist a research project at the London School of Economics. By
1922 he was lecturing on sociology, ethics and the history of political
ideas at the university and in 1929 succeeded Hobhouse as Professor
of Sociology, a position he held until 1954. A defining quality of his
work was his combination of social science and social philosophy
to create a general sociology. Ginsberg enjoyed studying the Jewish
people through a framework of sociology. In 1956 he produced *The
Jewish People Today*, in which he sought to elucidate how modern
Jewish society structured itself. He was also an editor of the *Jewish
Journal of Sociology* and a member of the World Jewish Congress.

Christian David Ginsburg

Expert on Biblical texts and
revealer of forgeries
1821 – 1914

Christian David Ginsburg was
considered to be a leading
expert in the interpretation of
the Masoretic text (the Hebrew
and Aramaic text of the Bible).
He was born in Poland to parents
who may have had connections to the Spanish court of Ferdinand
and Isabella. He received a traditional religious education and also
worked as a cotton spinner. In 1846, after coming under the influence
of the London Society for Promoting Christianity amongst Jews, he
converted to Christianity, took the name Christian and moved to
England where he trained as a missionary. Ginsburg distinguished
himself as a biblical scholar, writing commentaries on the *Song of
Solomon* and Ecclesiastes as well as a history of the Cabbala. He is
best known for his examination of the Masoretic text, which, after
extensive scholarship, culminated in a four-volume publication, *The
Massorah*. He was asked to contribute to the British and Foreign
Society's *New Critical Hebrew Bible*. In 1883 he saved the British
Museum from financial loss and humiliation when he proved that
newly discovered fragments of Deuteronomy, known as the Shapiro
fragments, were in fact forgeries.

Max Gluckman
Social anthropologist
1911–1975

Herman Max Gluckmann was born in Johannesburg, South Africa. His parents were Emmanuel Gluckmann, a lawyer, and his wife Kate Cohen, a leading Zionist. Gluckman, who dropped the final "n" from his name, was educated at King Edward VII School in Johannesburg and went on to the University of Witwatersrand in 1928. He intended to study law but was diverted into social anthropology and came down with a first-class degree. He was awarded the Transvaal Rhodes scholarship for 1934, and enrolled in Exeter College, Oxford. At Oxford he got his DPhil, and after a period of research was appointed to the staff of the Rhodes-Livingstone Institute in Rhodesia in 1939. Despite antisemitic opposition he became its director in 1942. In 1947 he returned to Oxford on a lectureship. In 1949 he moved to the University of Manchester to a specially established post, and remained there until his death. Gluckman is best remembered for his masterly researches in legal anthropology. In *The Judicial Process among the Barotse* (1955,1967) and *The Ideas in Barotse Jurisprudence* (1965,1972) he investigated the procedures and applied standards of Barotse tribal judiciary and found them directly comparable with western practice.

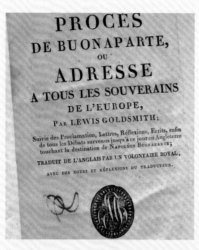

Lewis Goldsmith
Napoleon's secret agent
1763–1846

Lewis Goldsmith was born in
Surrey to parents from the
Sephardi community. The exact
year of his birth is unknown
as he was given to changing it
when it suited him. Similarly,
sources differ as to whether
the family was observant. Goldsmith had a colourful life, embroiled
in political intrigue and espionage. In 1792 he travelled to Europe,
where he witnessed the last few years of the Polish Republic. In
1801, Goldsmith wrote *Crimes of the Cabinet*, which accused the
British of insincerity during the peace talks that followed the war
between Poland and Russia. He subsequently travelled to Paris and
established the pro-Napoleonic paper *Argus*. Goldsmith was then
employed by Napoleon as a secret agent, charged with spying on
the Bourbon court. He was betrayed and fled France. Arriving back
in England in 1809, he was arrested for treason and imprisoned.
He wrote *The Secret History of the Cabinet of Bonaparte*, turning
on his former employer and calling for Napoleon's execution.
Historian Simon Burrows argues that all of Goldsmith's tales must be
approached with caution as the writer enjoyed embellishing a story
when he could. But what was a fault for a historian was an asset for a
journalist; Goldsmith was one of the first Jews to work successfully in
the London press.

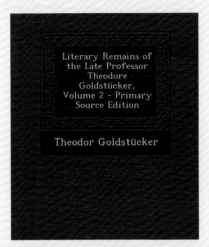

Literary Remains of
the Late Professor
Theodore
Goldstücker,
Volume 2 - Primary
Source Edition

Theodor Goldstücker

Theodor Goldstucker
Orientalist
1821–1872

Theodor H. Goldstucker was born in Konigsberg, Prussia. His father was a merchant. Goldstucker was educated at the Altstadtisches Gymnasium and Konigsberg University. In 1838 he moved to Bonn to study Indology, returning to Konigsberg to take his doctorate in 1840. After a brief period in Berlin, his liberal politics saw him banished and he moved to London in 1850. There in 1852 he took up the chair of Sanskrit at University College London. Goldstucker was widely respected for his learning in Sanskrit grammar, philosophy, lexicology and the theory of ritual (*purvamimamsa*), but he published little for so learned a scholar, holding himself to almost impossible standards of perfection. In 1856 he embarked on a revision of Wilson's dictionary, but after eight years and 480 pages had to abandon the project, having not even completed the entries for the first letter of the Sanskrit alphabet. His most famous work was a monograph of India's greatest grammarian Panini – *Panini: His Place in Sanskrit Literature* was published in 1861. Goldstucker was active in the Royal Asiatic Society and the East India Association. He was President of the Philological Society at the time of his death.

Hermann Gollancz
Rabbi and scholar
1852–1930

Hermann Gollancz was born in Bremen, Germany. He was the eldest son of Rabbi Samuel Marcus Gollancz, minister of the Hambro Synagogue in London, and his wife Johanna Koppell. He was educated at the Whitechapel foundation school, Jews' College and University College London. He graduated in Classics and philosophy in 1873 and was awarded his MA in Hebrew, Syriac and German in 1889. He began preaching in 1872 at his father's synagogue, and in 1892 he succeeded Chief Rabbi Hermann Adler as minister at the Bayswater Synagogue, Harrow Road. He remained there for a record 51 years in Anglo-Jewish ministry. Gollancz worked tirelessly for the foundation of new synagogues all over Britain. In 1902 he was elected Goldsmid Professor of Hebrew at University College London. When Adler died in 1911, Gollancz's claims to succeed him as chief rabbi were overruled in favour of a younger candidate. He remained at Bayswater and in 1915 published his translation of Joseph Kimhi's *Foundation of Religious Fear*. Gollancz undertook a great deal of public work outside the Jewish community. In 1917 he received an illuminated address on the completion of 45 years of service as a public worker, signed by numerous educational and philanthropic bodies. On his retirement from University College in 1923, he donated his considerable collection of Judaica to the college and was made Emeritus Professor. In the same year he was knighted, the first British rabbi to receive the honour.

Israel Gollancz

Shakespeare expert who
made the Bard accessible
1863–1930

Israel Gollancz was born in
London. His father, Rabbi Samuel
Gollancz, was the cantor of
the Hambro Synagogue and
raised Israel as an Orthodox Jew.
Israel's brother, Hermann, was a
rabbi and Hebrew scholar, while his nephew was Victor Gollancz the
publisher. Israel was a scholar at Christ's College, Cambridge, where
he studied medieval and modern languages. He became the first
lecturer of English at the university in 1896 before taking up what
would be a lifelong post as chair of English language and literature
at King's College London. Gollancz transformed the department
into one of the university's most significant faculties. He was also
a founder of the British Academy and played an important role in
the development of the National Theatre. Gollancz was a leading
scholar on Shakespeare and collated many different responses to the
playwright's work in *The Book of Homage to Shakespeare* (1916). He
also sought to make the Bard's works more accessible to the public
through the pocket-size Temple Shakespeare editions. Gollancz was
knighted in 1919. The British Academy awards a biennial prize for
English literature in his name.

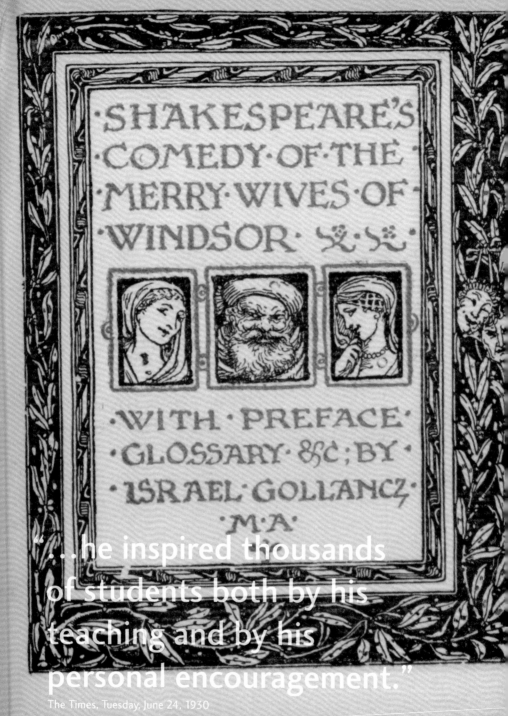

·SHAKESPEARE'S·
COMEDY·OF·THE·
MERRY·WIVES·OF·
WINDSOR·

·WITH·PREFACE·
·GLOSSARY·&c;·BY·
·ISRAEL·GOLLANCZ·
·M·A·

·MDCCCC·PUBLISHED·BY·J·M·DENT·
·AND·CO:·ALDINE·HOUSE·LONDON·E·C

"...he inspired thousands of students both by his teaching and by his personal encouragement."

The Times, Tuesday, June 24, 1930

Ernst Gombrich
Introduced millions
to art history
1909–2001

Ernst Gombrich was born in
Vienna, Austria. Although his
parents were Jewish, they both
converted to Protestantism
and Ernst followed suit. He
developed his passion for art
history at Vienna University, writing an innovative dissertation on the
psychological context of Giulio Romano's Palazzo del Te. Gombrich
expanded and published his research in two journal articles in 1934
and 1935, leading to a collaboration with the art historian Ernst Kris.
Gombrich was forced to abandon the project to escape the growing
Nazi threat in 1936, and he moved to England to take up a research
role at the Warburg Institute. In 1950 Gombrich published *The
Story of Art*, a book designed as an introduction to art for children
but which has since been read by millions of adults throughout the
world. Gombrich proceeded to turn the field on its head with *Art and
Illusion* (1960) by interrogating the role of perception in art. The
two works established Gombrich as "the best known art historian
in Britain". During the Second World War he was employed in the
monitoring department of the BBC World Service and was the first to
break the news to Churchill of Hitler's death.

Arthur Lehman Goodhart

Legal academic and professor
1891 – 1978

Arthur Lehman Goodhart was born in New York City and was educated at Hotchkiss School, Yale University and Trinity College, Cambridge. He became a barrister in 1919 and went on to teach law at Cambridge, becoming a fellow of Corpus Christi College. In 1931 he became Professor of Jurisprudence at Oxford until 1951 when he became Master of University College, Oxford. Goodhart was a founder and editor of the *Cambridge Law Journal* in 1921 and then editor of the *Law Quarterly Review* for 46 years. Goodhart used his position to argue for law reform. He became a King's Counsel in 1942 and was made an honorary Knight of the British Empire in 1948 for promoting the cause of Anglo-American understanding through lecture tours. He became a fellow of the British Academy in 1952 and received honorary degrees from 20 universities. Goodhart was a non-practising Jew who married a devout Anglican but took an interest in Jewish affairs. He wrote about the Jews after visiting Poland in 1919, and gave lectures for Jewish organisations. He supported Israel's determination not to relinquish Arab territories without adequate safeguards and advocated stern measure against terrorism. He was also President of the Pedestrians Association.

Jean Gottmann

Geographer
1915–1994

Jean Gottmann was born in Kharkov in Ukraine. His parents, Elie Gottmann and Sonia-Fanny Ettinger, were killed in 1918, following the Russian Revolution. Gottmann escaped to Paris in the company of his aunt and uncle. There he found employment as a research assistant in economic geography at the Sorbonne in 1937. In 1940, following Nazi occupation, he was banned from public employment and fled to the United States. He received a Rockefeller Foundation fellowship to study at Princeton. During the war he consulted for the Board of Economic Welfare, and in 1945 he returned to France to work for the Ministry of the Economy and the United Nations. After the war he commuted between France and the United States. He produced a regional study of Virginia with the aid of a grant from Paul Mellon. He received financial support from the Century Foundation to embark on his life's great work: the study of the megalopolis of the north-eastern seaboard of the United States. In 1968 he became Professor of Geography and head of department at the School of Geography at the University of Oxford, where he spent the rest of his career. After retiring as Emeritus Professor in 1983 he remained in Oxford for the rest of his life.

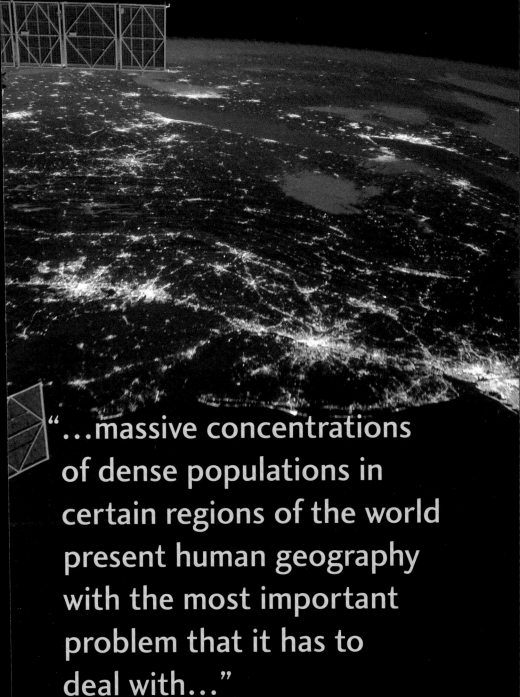

"...massive concentrations of dense populations in certain regions of the world present human geography with the most important problem that it has to deal with..."

Richard Gottheil
Historian and Zionist
1862–1936

Richard James Horatio Gottheil was born in Manchester, England. He was educated at Chorlton High School. At the age of 11 he moved to the United States when his father Gustav Gottheil was offered the position of assistant rabbi of Temple Emanu-El in New York. He attended Columbia College and graduated in 1881, taking his MA at the University of Leipzig in 1886. In 1877 he was elected to the chair of rabbinical literature at Columbia University. From 1898 to 1904 he was president of the American Federation of Zionists, and attended the Basel Zionist Congresses of 1898, 1899 and 1903. From 1904 he was vice-president of the American Jewish Historical Society. He also served as chief of the Oriental Department of the New York Public Library. Gottheil wrote numerous articles on oriental and Jewish questions for newspapers and periodicals. He published some significant texts on the Syriac language, including *The Syriac Grammar of Mar Elia Zobha* (1887) and *Selections from the Syriac Julian Romance* (1906). Gottheil was one of the editors of the *Jewish Encyclopedia*.

Hugo Gryn

Rabbi and presenter
of *The Moral Maze*
1930–1996

Hugo Gabriel Gryn was
born in Berehovo, in former
Czechoslovakia, into a family
with a love of learning. His
parents were Geza Gryn, a
timber merchant, and Bella
Neufeld. Gryn cheated death twice in his early years, surviving both
the gas chambers of Auschwitz and the death march from Lieberose
to Sachsenhausen. Gryn was flown out of Prague by the Central
British Fund, and was sent to live near Edinburgh. He was educated
at Polton House farm school before winning a scholarship to King's
College Cambridge, graduating in mathematics and chemistry in
1948. In 1950 he went to the Hebrew Union College in Cincinnati,
where he was ordained in 1957. In 1964 he became first associate
and then senior rabbi of the West London Synagogue, a post he
held until his death. As a religious thinker, he considerably influenced
the development of the Reform liturgy, chairing the group that
produced *Forms of Prayer* (1977) and *Forms of Prayer 3: Prayers for
the High Holidays* (1985). He became beloved of the British public
through his radio broadcasts on BBC Radio, *Thought for the Day*,
Pause for Thought and *The Moral Maze*. Gryn's theological reflections
were recorded in *Chasing Shadows* (2000), a memoir written by his
daughter Naomi Gryn after his death.

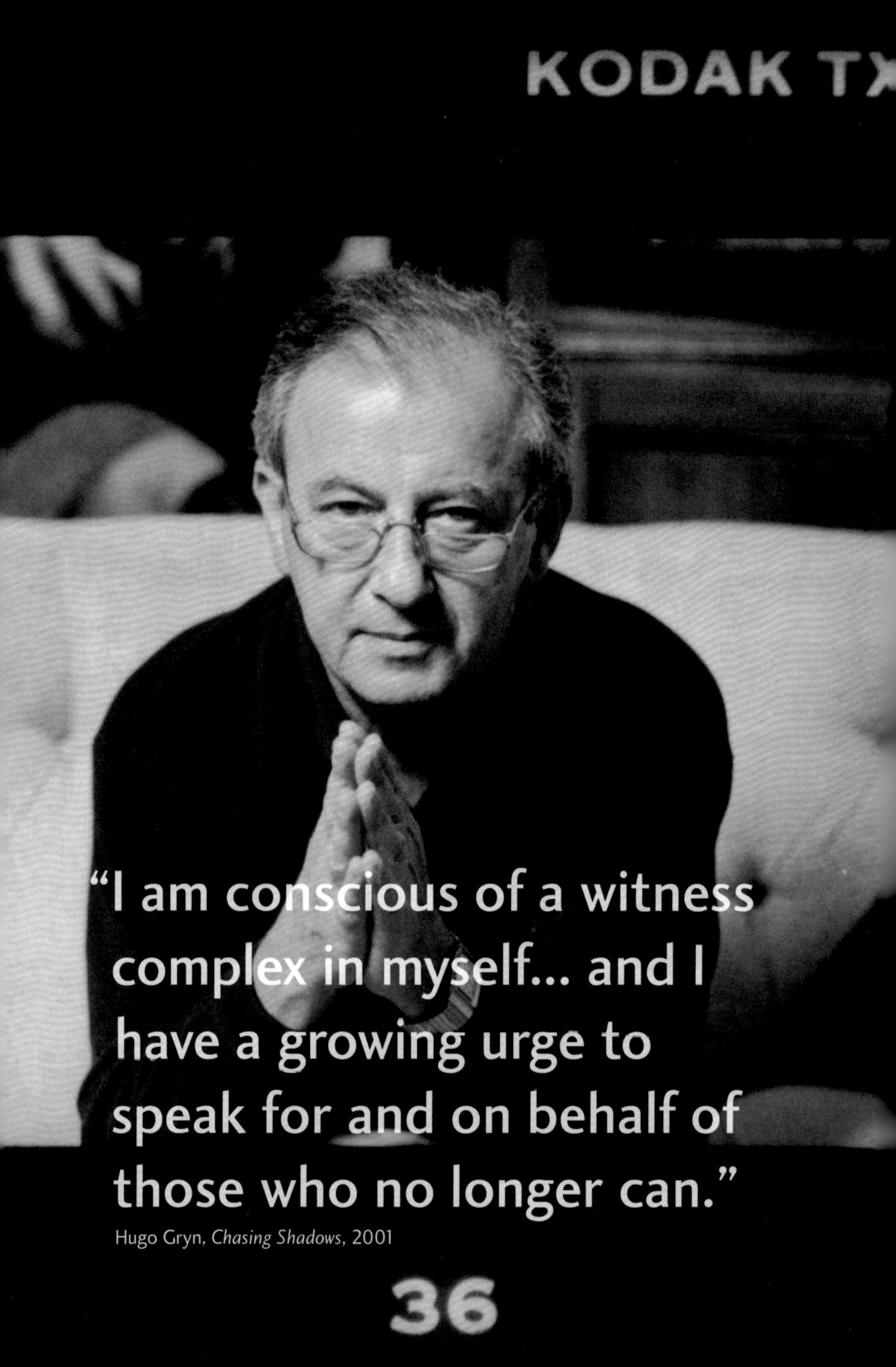

"I am conscious of a witness complex in myself... and I have a growing urge to speak for and on behalf of those who no longer can."

Hugo Gryn, *Chasing Shadows*, 2001

Philip Guedalla

Biographer, historian
and essayist
1889–1944

Philip Guedalla was born in
Maida Vale, London to an
English family of Spanish and
Portuguese descent. His father
David was a pioneer English
Zionist. He was educated at
Rugby School and Balliol College, Oxford, where he was President
of the Oxford Union. He worked as a barrister for ten years before
turning his hand to the writing of biographies. He was described as
one of the most popular biographers of his time. He is best known
for his books *Palmerston, The Duke* (Wellington), *The Queen and
Mr Gladstone* and *Mr Churchill*. He described biography as "a very
definite region bounded on the north by history, on the south by
fiction, on the east by obituary, and on the west by tedium." While
he principally wrote English biographies, he also wrote French ones
on Napoleon III, Bazaine and Petain. He was active in politics and
unsuccessfully stood as a Liberal candidate for parliament several
times. Guedalla was President of the British Zionist Federation,
served as president of the Jewish Historical Society of England and
was Vice-President of the Jewish Representative Council. He was a
popular speaker and lecturer. He was a member of the Spanish and
Portuguese Synagogue and married Nellie Reitlinger. He died the
day after the publication of his book *Middle East, 1940–42: A Study
in Air Power* and was buried at the Golders Green Jewish Cemetery.

Kurt Hahn

Led an education revolution
1886–1974

Kurt Matthias Robert Martin Hahn was born in Berlin, educated at the Wilhelmsgymnasium and then spent two years at Christ Church College, Oxford. In the First World War Hahn served as a German intelligence operative, and in this capacity he became acquainted with Prince Max of Baden. The pair discovered a shared belief in the need for holistic education and decided to found a boarding school housed in the prince's castle at Salem. In 1933 the school received a valuable endorsement when Prince Philip of Greece enrolled there. Hitler's rise to power, however, made Hahn's position as a Jewish headmaster untenable. He was briefly imprisoned and released on the intervention of the British prime minister Ramsay MacDonald. Hahn settled in Britain and in 1934, with the support of powerful British establishment figures including novelist John Buchan and historian G. W. Trevelyan, founded Gordonstoun School on the Moray coast in Scotland. Prince Philip joined the school in 1934 and remained there for five years. He later sent his sons Charles, Andrew and Edward there. Prince Philip agreed so wholeheartedly with Hahn's ideas of educating the whole person that he instituted his Duke of Edinburgh's award scheme. Hahn became a British citizen in 1938 and was baptised into the Church of England in 1945. He retired as headmaster of Gordonstoun in 1953 and was appointed CBE in 1964.

"There is more in
you than you think."

Motto of Kurt Hahn, founder of Gordonstoun School and mentor to Prince Philip,
pictured here at the school in a 1935 production of *Macbeth*.

Charlotte Haldane
One of the first women
on Fleet Street
1894–1969

Charlotte Haldane was born in
south London to Joseph Franken
and wife Mathilde. Her parents
had emigrated from Germany
in order to strengthen Joseph's
fur business. In 1906 Haldane
moved to Antwerp, where she experienced strong antisemitism. The
family returned to England but faced more persecution when her
father Joseph was classed as an enemy alien in the run-up to the
First World War. Haldane began her career as a reporter for the *Daily
Express* in 1920. Her articles were controversial, calling for divorce
reform, access to contraception and the right for women to work.
Her work in support of women's causes later led to her becoming
the editor of the anti-fascist magazine *Women Today.* She was one of
the first women on Fleet Street, but as her father had taught her to
"drink like a man," Charlotte held her own. Following Hitler's rise to
power, Haldane became a strong supporter of the Communist Party.
She travelled to Spain with Paul Robeson to support the Republican
forces. During the Second World War, Haldane was the only
woman on the first British war convoy to Russia, where she became
disillusioned with communism. For a time, she worked with George
Orwell on the BBC's Eastern Service. Haldane was not religiously
observant. She was married twice, to non-Jewish men, in Church of
England wedding ceremonies.

Aaron Hart

First Chief Rabbi of the
United Kingdom
1670–1756

Aaron Hart was born in
Breslau, Germany. He was
the son of Hartwig Moses
Hart, Breslau's rabbi. He
was educated at yeshivot in
Poland, and moved to England
sometime after 1657, following his merchant brother Moses. In
1705 Aaron succeeded Jehuda Loeb as the rabbi of the Ashkenazi
community at the synagogue in Shoemaker's Row. In 1707 he
wrote *Urim v'tumin*, a spirited defence of his excommunication of
another rabbi, Marcus Moses. It was the only book he ever wrote;
it was also the first book to be printed in Hebrew in London. In
1721 Hart's synagogue moved to a new building in Duke's Place,
Aldgate, which had been financed by his brother. There he was
petitioned by Edward Goldney, who had embarked upon a mission
to convert Jews to Christianity and concentrated his efforts on
prominent members of the community. Hart rebutted Goldney's
attempts, declaring that the Jewish religion had been singled out
for conversion. "If it had been his fortune to have been born and
bred a Mahometan," he said, "or in the principles of any other
religion, he should have continued as such." Hart remained at the
synagogue until his death.

H. L. A. Hart

He made complex legal ideas
easily understandable
1907–1992

Herbert Lionel Hart was born
in Harrogate to garment
traders Simeon and Rose. His
parents were German and Polish
immigrants. Hart was educated
at Bradford Grammar School
and New College Oxford, where he took a congratulatory first in
classical greats. He became a barrister and practised at Chancery
Bar between 1932 and 1940. During the Second World War, Hart
worked for MI5 at Bletchley Park and was a colleague of Alan
Turing. After the war Hart did not practise law again but turned to
teaching, accepting a fellowship at New College Oxford, his *alma
mater*. He wrote *The Concept of Law*, in which he outlined two sets
of laws governing civilised society: primary laws, such as those
found in a country's legal system, and secondary laws that enforce
the primary ones. The work was the culmination of eight years of
lectures. Hart was then commissioned to write a new series of books
for the University Press, *The Clarendon Law Series*, which explained
the main issues of jurisprudence in jargon-free language. He also
lobbied for changes in the laws relating to homosexuality, claiming
that the reforms following the Wolfenden report of 1957 "didn't go
far enough". In his younger days, Hart was ambivalent towards his
Jewish heritage. However, a visit to Jerusalem in 1964 renewed his
appreciation for his Orthodox upbringing. He claimed that without
Jerusalem, life would be a "howling wilderness."

Ernest Abraham Hart

He championed public health
reform in the Victorian age
1835–1898

Ernest Abraham Hart was born
in London. His father was a
dentist and encouraged his
son's medical ambitions. Hart
was awarded a scholarship
that entitled him to study at
Cambridge. However, as a Jew he was subject to entry conditions
and he decided to forgo a university career. Instead, he studied
medicine at St George's Hospital, London. He qualified as a surgeon
in 1856 and specialised in ophthalmic surgery. He is best known
for his medical journalism and was appointed to the staff of the
Lancet in 1858. Later, Hart was appointed editor of the British
Medical Association's mouthpiece, the *British Medical Journal*. He
was responsible for increasing the readership of the journal on
a national scale. He wrote extensively on the subject of women's
health, infant health and better treatment for the poor. As chairman
of the Parliamentary Bills Committee he also oversaw many health
reform acts. Hart was outspoken about his faith and wrote *The
Mosaic Code* in 1877 about medical issues within the Torah. He
survived many attempts to oust him from his editorship of the *BMJ*;
it is difficult to determine whether this was due to antisemitism, or
was merely the reaction to his notoriously difficult personality.

Paula Heimann
Psychoanalyst
1899–1982

Paula Gertrude Klatzko was born in Danzig, Poland. Her parents were Russian. She trained at several German universities, taking her MD in 1928 in Berlin. While at Berlin she married Franz Heimann, a specialist in internal medicine. In 1932, following a period of analysis herself, she qualified as an associate member of the Berlin Psycho-Analytic Society. Heimann was implicated in the Reichstag fire of 1933; the fact that she had given a party on the night of the fire was seen as an act of complicity. She was arrested but later released, and fled to England shortly afterward, settling in London. She obtained British medical qualifications and was elected to full membership of the British Psychoanalytical Society in 1939. She was courted by Melanie Klein as a confidante and disciple, and the two women were considered to have an intense and not entirely healthy mother–daughter relationship. In the 1940s Heimann made a bid for freedom that left her traumatised. Her paper "On counter-transference" (1950), later seen as a major contribution to psychoanalysis, negated some of Klein's theories, and enraged her former mentor. In 1955 Heimann officially resigned from the Melanie Klein Trust. Heimann's legacy is often overshadowed by the sheer force of Klein's reputation, but her theories on counter-transference continue to impact upon the relationship between analyst and patient to this day.

Basil Henriques

Tank hero who inspired the
youth of London's East End
1890–1961

Basil Henriques was born in
London. His parents, David
and Agnes, were Sephardi Jews
whose ancestors had lived
in Jamaica before settling in
England. The family were early
champions of Reform Judaism and supported assimilation. Henriques
was educated at Harrow School and the University of Oxford. On
the outbreak of the First World War he joined the Tank Corps,
and served at the Battle of Flers-Courcelette in 1916, which saw
the first use of tanks on the battlefield. He served bravely in many
other battles, sustaining serious facial injuries following a direct hit
to his tank. After the Armistice Henriques found his life's vocation:
youth work. He worked with impoverished boys in London's East
End. These boys, often immigrants from eastern Europe, spoke little
English and held to strong religious practices. Henriques founded
the *Oxford and St George's Jewish Lads Club* in 1914. The club provided
education, vocational training, recreation and holidays in the
country and promoted Henriques' progressive vision of religion and
assimilation. His wife, Rose opened a girls' counterpart, *Oxford and
St George's Jewish Girls Club,* a year later. The club greatly expanded
and he remained as warden until 1947. Henriques later worked as
a magistrate, dealing with young offenders whom he thought were
missing the guiding hand of Judaism. Henriques was recognised for
his tireless youth work in 1955 when he received a knighthood.

Ridley Haim Herschell

Became one of England's best known missionaries
1807–1864

Ridley Haim Herschell was born to a very observant Jewish family in Poland. His grandfather, Rabbi Hillel, lived with them and had a profound influence on Ridley, who declared he too wanted to be a rabbi. However, in early adult life he moved to Paris, where he began to seriously question his faith. In 1830 he travelled to London, where he was baptised into the Church of England by the Bishop of London. Thereafter he dedicated his time to missionary work in London and the south-east of England. He established the British Society for the Propagation of the Gospel Amongst Jews as well as the Evangelical Alliance. He also travelled to Europe and America for his missionary work. Although Herschell clearly moved away from his Jewish heritage, he was respected for his view that the Old Testament should never be interpreted as merely an introduction to the New Testament. He also retained his middle name Haim, which is Hebrew for life, which his mother had given him after her near-death experience at the hands of French occupiers of her small town. His son, Farrer Herschell, became the first Jewish Lord Chancellor.

Joseph Hertz

Chief Rabbi

1872–1946

Joseph Herman Hertz was born in Rebrin, Slovakia, then part of Hungary. His parents were Simon Hertz and Esther Fanny Moskowitz. Hertz was educated at New York City College and gained his doctorate at Columbia University. He became the first rabbinic graduate of the Jewish Theological Seminary in New York in 1894. He became the rabbi of Syracuse, New York, and then in 1898 accepted the rabbinate of the Witwatersrand Old Hebrew Congregation in Johannesburg. In 1913 Hertz was chosen to be Hermann Adler's successor as Chief Rabbi of the United Hebrew Congregations of the British Empire, in preference to Hermann Gollancz. Hertz accepted the appointment and became a naturalised British citizen in 1915. He was a religious Zionist and his support of the Balfour Declaration in 1917 was considered to be hugely influential. In 1920 he embarked on an 11-month tour of the Jewish communities of the British Empire. Hertz clashed frequently with Sir Robert Waley-Cohen, president of the United Synagogue, ferociously criticising the more radical Liberal Synagogue. Deeply shaken by the fate of the Jews in the Second World War, Hertz lobbied for the rights of refugees to enter Palestine. He was committed to a dialogue between religions, and in 1942 he became founder president of the Council of Christians and Jews. Hertz was made a Companion of Honour in 1943.

Shmuel Yitzchak Hillman

Rabbi and scholar

1868–1953

Shmuel Yitzchak Hillman was born in Kovno, Lithuania. His parents were Paya Rivka and Avraham Chaim Hillman. He was educated in the Torah by his two uncles Rabbi Mordecai Hillman and Rabbi Noach Yaakov Hillman.

Later he received semicha – rabbinical ordination – from Rabbi Eliyahu Dovid Teumim, who was head of the Beth Din in Ponevezh and later Jerusalem. At the age of 29, in 1897, Hillman became rabbi and head of the Beth Din of Berazino in Minsk, Russia. In 1908 he settled in Glasgow, founding the Beth Din there and serving as rabbi. In 1914 he was appointed a dayan of the London Beth Din. On his retirement in 1934 he settled in Jerusalem, where he concentrated on writing and study. He co-founded Ohel Torah – the Jerusalem yeshiva – with his son-in-law and Chief Rabbi of Israel Yitzhak HaLevi Herzog, and served there as its rosh yeshiva. His grandson was Chaim Herzog, president of Israel, and his grandson politician Isaac Herzog.

Solomon Hirschell
Chief Rabbi
1762–1842

Solomon Hirschell was born in London. He was the youngest son of Hart Lyon, rabbi of the Great Synagogue in Duke's Place, London, and his wife Golda. Hirschell received a traditional Jewish education in Poland, where he became an able Talmudic scholar. Thereafter he embarked on a rabbinic career and took up a position in Prenzlau, Prussia. In 1802 Hirschell was elected to the position of rabbi of the Great Synagogue. He never mastered the English language and his sermon giving thanks for the British victory at Trafalgar had to be translated into English from Yiddish. As Ashkenazi Jews far outnumbered Sephardim in Britain at the time of Hirschell's appointment, he became known as the natural spokesperson for all British Jews, and thus became first Chief Rabbi of the British Empire. He was in office for 40 years, and in the print press was dubbed the "high priest" of Anglo-Jewry. In 1840 he founded a Reform congregation in London; but, as an eastern-European rabbi of the old school, he had no real appetite for change, and it was left to his successors to effect real reform.

Paul Hirst

Sociologist
1946–2003

Paul Quentin Hirst was born in
Holberton, Devon. His father
was Henry Hirst, a fitter in the
car trade, and his wife Joyce
Evelyn Schaffer. Henry joined
the RAF and rose through
the ranks to officer class,
so Paul was educated at a series of military schools in Germany,
settling at last at Plymouth Grammar School. He took up a place
at Leicester University to read sociology. There he studied under
German refugee and fellow Jew Norbert Elias. In 1968 he moved
to the University of Sussex to read for his MA. In 1969 he was
appointed lecturer at Birkbeck College, where he proved a brilliant
teacher, ending almost every pronouncement with an interrogative
"Right?!" In 1975 Hirst published *Pre-Capitalist Modes of Production*,
following this work with *Marx's "Capital" and Capitalism Today*. In
1985 he was appointed to a chair of social theory at Birkbeck. He
was a prominent figure in the Fabian Society. He wrote 18 books
and hundreds of articles on a wide range of subjects that fell within
his sphere of expertise. Hirst was always eager to think afresh and
tackle new problems. He wrote: "To be engaged and try to be
objective is tough, but it is the only serious stance."

Christopher Hitchens
Writer and public intellectual
1949–2011

Born in Portsmouth and graduating from Balliol College with a degree in philosophy, politics and economics, Hitchens would become perhaps the most celebrated public intellectual of his generation. Over a career in journalism that began in the UK and continued after his move to the United States in 1981, Hitchens' work appeared in dozens of publications including *the New Statesman*, the *Nation* and *Vanity Fair*. Combining a love of literature with an appetite for argument, Hitchens gained a reputation for his polemics against figures as diverse as Mother Teresa, Bill Clinton and Henry Kissinger. For years a Trotskyist and opponent of imperialism, Hitchens broke with most of the left to support the wars with Afghanistan and Iraq. It was during these years that Hitchens became known for his public debates and numerous appearances on television. Having acquired such a large platform, Hitchens used it to become a leading advocate of atheism, and would publish his best-known full-length work, *God Is Not Great*, in 2007. This was followed in 2010 by the memoir *Hitch-22*. Notable collections of Hitchens' journalism include *For the Sake of Argument* (1993), *Love, Poverty, and War* (2004) and *Arguably* (2011). Hitchens learned his mother was Jewish only after her death, and came to view himself as Jewish insofar as he welcomed the opportunity to defy antisemites.

Philip Hobsbaum
Became a "servant to the
makers" of poetry
1932–2005

Philip Hobsbaum was born
in Whitechapel, London. He
was raised in a Polish-Jewish
family who moved to Bradford,
Yorkshire when he was seven.
During his time at Belle Vue
Grammar School, Hobsbaum regularly debated at the Jewish society.
He read English at Downing College, Cambridge and edited the
student magazine *Delta*. He had an eye for literary talent, publishing
early poems by Ted Hughes and Peter Redgrove. Hobsbaum himself
also wrote poetry and established a recital society called the
Cambridge Group. The meetings continued as the Group when
Hobsbaum moved to London, and played host to some of Britain's
finest poets. Hobsbaum's own poetry was being published in
magazines of the day but it was through these writing workshops that
he made his greatest contribution to the arts, by providing support
and constructive criticism to young poets. Seamus Heaney, Nobel
Prize winner, credited the Belfast workshop as a formative experience
in his literary career. In 1963 Hobsbaum edited and published *A
Group Anthology*, a collection of poems discussed at the workshops.
He also had an extensive output of literary criticism. Hobsbaum was
an atheist and identified with England more than his Jewish roots, but
always felt like an outsider. Among his students at Tulse Hill school
was a young Ken Livingstone, later Mayor of London.

Eric Hobsbawm

Influential historian of 19th- and 20th-century Europe
1917–2012

Eric Hobsbawm was born in Alexandria, Egypt to Polish parents. The family moved to Austria but Hobsbawm and his sister were orphaned as teenagers and moved to live with relatives in Berlin. The rise of the Nazi Party in 1933 meant leaving for Britain and Hobsbawm later commented that seeing Hitler at close hand "made me a lifelong communist." Hobsbawm charted the history of two centuries of modern Europe in *The Age of Revolution: 1789–1848* (1962), *The Age of Capital: 1848–1875*, (1975), *The Age of Empire: 1875–1914*, (1987) and *The Age of Extremes: the Short Twentieth Century 1914–1991* (1994). He wove together political, cultural and economic strands in an easily accessible style for the general reader. A brilliant academic, lecturer and observer of social trends, Hobsbawm applied his towering intellect to the political issues of the day and his Marxist approach to the history of the British working class became influential among left-wing activists in the 1960s and 70s. The family did not observe Jewish religious rituals and Hobsbawm called himself a "non-Jewish Jew". However, his mother drummed into him "whatever you do, never deny you are Jewish" and he requested that the Kaddish be recited at his funeral. Eric Hobsbawm is, fittingly, buried near Karl Marx in Highgate Cemetery.

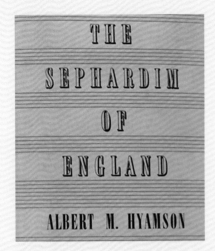

THE SEPHARDIM OF ENGLAND

ALBERT M. HYAMSON

Albert Montefiore Hyamson
British civil servant, historian and "spiritual" Zionist
1874–1954

Albert Montefiore Hyamson was born in London. His father was from Russian Poland. Hyamson joined the civil service and during the First World War began working for the Jewish Bureau in the Department of Information. It was a role that allowed Hyamson to distribute propaganda promoting Zionism and emphasise British support. In the pamphlet *Great Britain and the Jews*, he stated that the Balfour Declaration was part of a long tradition of British sympathy for the Jews. In 1921 he was put in charge of the Palestinian Administration's immigration department and made decisions on many of the applications personally, which unfortunately caused such a backlog that he was removed from his post. This and his support for a single state for Jews and Arabs with equal rights and autonomy made him unpopular. Hyamson called himself a "spiritual Zionist" rather than a nationalist or political Zionist. He believed in limits on land sales to Jews and immigration so that Jews did not constitute more than 50 per cent of the population. He was a member of the Union of Jewish Literary Societies and the Jewish Fellowship, a fellow of the Royal Historical Society and President of the Jewish Historical Society of England.

Moses Hyamson
Rabbi and scholar
1862–1949

Moses Hyamson was born in Suvalk, Russia, now in Poland. In 1864 he emigrated to England, where he was educated in the Talmud by his father, Rabbi Nathan Haimsohn. Hyamson went on to Jews' College, London, and University College London. He received a BA in 1882, followed by a Bachelor of Laws in 1900 and a doctorate in 1912. He was ordained as a rabbi by Rabbi Hermann Adler at Jews' College. He served as a rabbi in Swansea and Bristol before settling in London, where he was appointed rabbi in Dalston and a dayan of the London Beth Din. He was a potential candidate for the post of Chief Rabbi of the British Empire, losing out to Joseph Hertz. In 1913 Hyamson was elected to a post in New York as rabbi of Congregation Orach Chaim. He replaced Hertz, to whom he had lost the British appointment. His was a life contract and he served until his death. In 1914 Hyamson founded the Board of Milah, and he was an early leader of the Union of Orthodox Jewish Congregations of America. He was committed to education, founding a local Hebrew school and supporting European yeshivas. Hyamson believed in the fixity of the Sabbath, and campaigned to prevent the holy day "wandering" to a different day of the week each year.

"Owners of capital will stimulate working class to buy more and more of expensive goods, houses and technology, pushing them to take more and more expensive credits, until their debt becomes unbearable."

Karl Marx

Karl Marx and Anglo-Jewish thought

Karl Marx Hof in Vienna, Austria, is the longest single residential building in the world. Built in 1930 it became one of the main battlefields of the brief Austrian civil war of 1934 when the outlawed paramilitary group Republikanischer Schutzbund barricaded themselves inside.

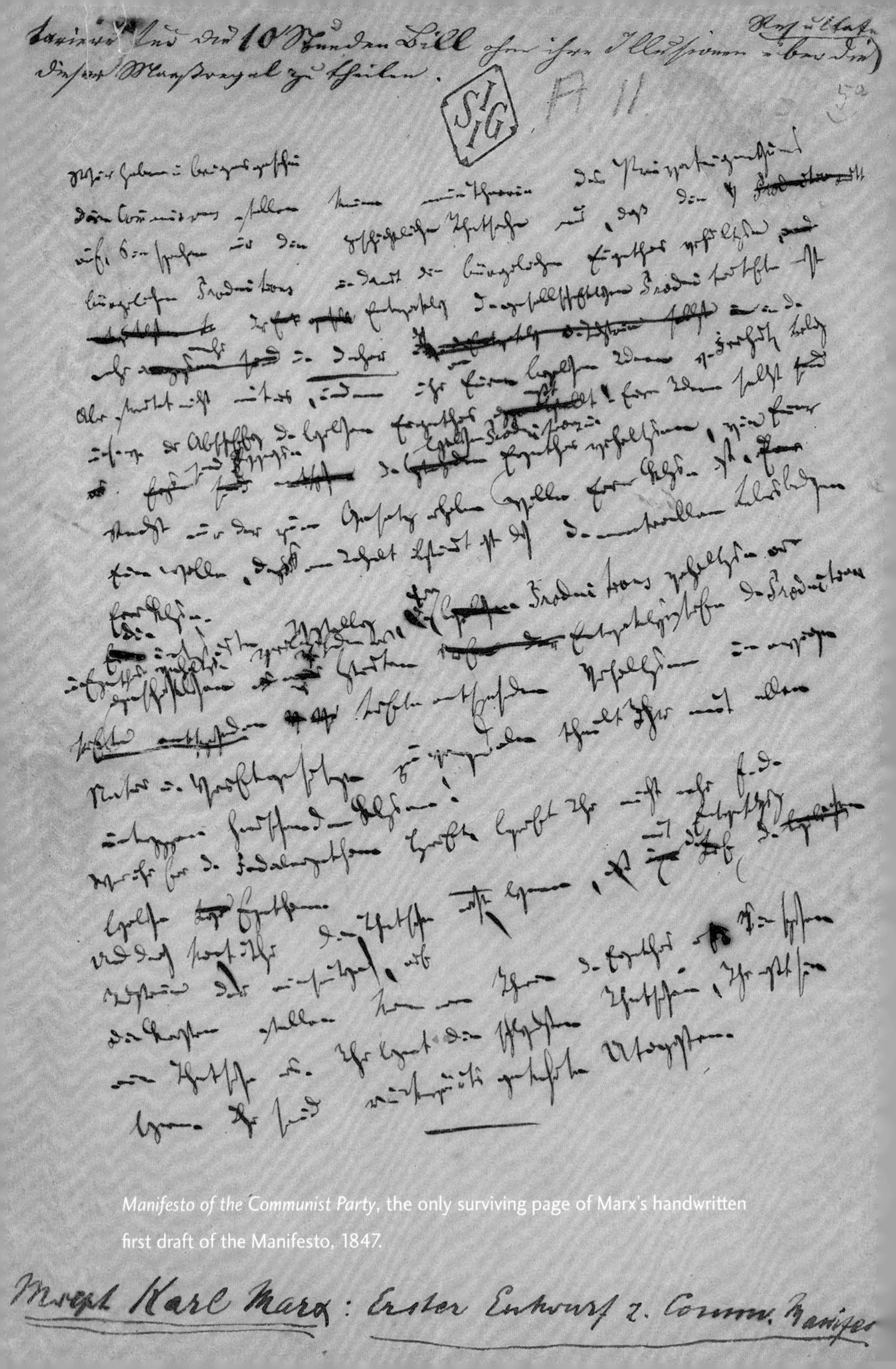

Manifesto of the Communist Party, the only surviving page of Marx's handwritten first draft of the Manifesto, 1847.

Joseph Karl Marx: Erster Entwurf z. Comm. Manifes

Karl Marx and Anglo-Jewish thought

David Rosenberg
Writer and tour guide on London's radical history

Karl Marx never went to *shul* (synagogue) despite both his parents being descended from a long line of rabbis. I blame his father, the lawyer Herschel Marx, born in Saarlautern in 1782, who later settled in Trier, a town of 12,000 people by the Moselle, where his brother Samuel was the senior rabbi. In 1817 Herschel the Jew became Heinrich the (Lutheran) Protestant, to sidestep barriers blocking his career. Why did Herschel choose Protestantism in heavily Catholic Trier? Perhaps he still enjoyed being a minority.

Herschel and Henrietta Marx had nine children. Only four survived to adulthood. Karl Marx was born in 1818. Since Judaism is passed down by the mother, and Henrietta postponed her baptism until after her father's death in 1825, Karl was officially born a Jew. Not for too long, though. He was baptised at the age of six. Then, as a young adult, Karl dispensed with both Lutheranism and Judaism and declared himself an atheist. He memorably described religion, in 1844, as "the opiate of the masses". It comforted people, he said. It relieved pain in their lives and gave them temporary euphoria and pleasant illusions. But he wanted people to ditch their illusions, confront reality and change the world.

I was never offered opiates in *shul* I when I was young. We were lucky to get a boiled sweet from the shamash. I don't recall much praying either. Instead I heard *sotto voce* discussions of football, horse-racing and business worries, interspersed with the congregants standing up, singing like an unruly football crowd or muttering Hebrew words at lightning speed. "In *shul,*" one Jewish Marxist told me, "people pray to a God they don't believe in, in a language they don't understand, for the security of a state they don't want to live in."

On my wedding day, though, Karl Marx the Jew was proudly namechecked by Rabbi Bayfield, head of the Reform Synagogue Movement as he generously described me and my partner, Julia, as social justice campaigners within a "Jewish prophetic tradition", stretching from Amos and Mica via Marx to the present. The mere mention of Marx provoked nervous coughs among some relatives.

But Marx was indeed a prophet, who argued that major historical changes resulted from the struggle for ascendancy between antagonistic socio-economic classes. In 1818, when Marx was born, the old landed aristocracy were being challenged by a rising industrial bourgeoisie. Once the bourgeoisie triumphed, though, they could only sustain their dominance through economically exploiting the class that filled its factories – the "proletariat". It was inevitable, Marx believed, that one day the proletariat would revolt, seize power in the name of the majority and establish a society based on equality and justice.

When Marx first visited London in 1845 he met German migrant workers and leaders of radical political groups. On his second visit, in 1847, one group – the Communist League – commissioned him to distil his revolutionary ideas in an accessible pamphlet that would inspire the proletariat to fulfil its historic role. He collaborated on this with Friedrich Engels, and in 1848 they published *The Communist Manifesto*. It has never been out of print. I possess a Yiddish copy, published by the Jewish Socialist Bund in 1919 in Warsaw. It begins: "*A ruakh, a shotn geyt arum iber ayrope – der shotn fun komunizm.*" (A spirit, a spectre, is haunting Europe – the spectre of communism). The pamphlet urges workers to launch themselves into the struggle: "You have nothing to lose but your chains. You have a world to win." It closes with the rallying cry: "Workers of the World Unite!"

The Marx family settled permanently in London in 1849, living temporarily in Camberwell and Chelsea before renting a two-room flat in Soho, an area full of exiled revolutionaries. Later, they lived in Kentish Town.

Most Jewish Londoners at that time would have scoffed at his manifesto. A small influx of poorer Jews from Holland and Germany scraped a living as clothing and cigarette makers, small traders or petty criminals, but heads of Jewish households were more typically bankers, stockbrokers and entrepreneurs living in capitalist comfort, though barred from standing as MPs until 1858, and their children could not study at Oxford or Cambridge Universities until 1856.

By the time Marx died in London, in 1883, having written *Das Kapital*, pauperised Jews from the Russian Empire were pouring into Britain, fleeing pogroms and persecution. Marx's vision of a just world, where the downtrodden and persecuted would turn the tables, spoke directly to Jewish migrants working 14–18 hour shifts for subsistence level pay in dingy East End sweatshops. They came to view their situation not as a misfortune but as an injustice that they could remedy through forming unions and striking for better conditions against the sweatshop owners. The banner of the Jewish Trouser Makers' Union, formed in 1882, was emblazoned with Marx's slogan: "Workers of the World Unite!" in English and Yiddish.

Marx had his greatest influence on British Jews between the 1880s and the 1930s. Some joined the early radical and revolutionary groups, such as the Social Democratic Federation and the Socialist League, and studied his economic teachings. Bundist exiles in London campaigned in Yiddish, keeping workers informed about developments in Russia while preparing them for struggle in their workplaces here. East End anarchists organised around a Yiddish newspaper, *Arbeter Fraynd,* which embraced Marx's economics

Battle of Cable Street, anti-fascist groups clashed with members of the British Union of Fascists, led by Oswald Mosley, in London on October 1936.

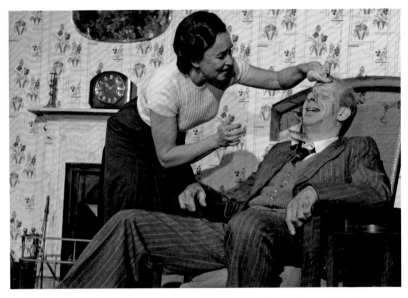

Arnold Wesker, Samantha Spiro and Steve Furst star in *Chicken Soup with Barley*, Royal Court Theatre, London, 2011.

but leaned closer to utopian political thinkers such as Proudhon and Bakunin.

Marx's youngest daughter Eleanor admired her father's work and was active in the Bloomsbury Socialist Society that met in the "Communist Club". She proudly reclaimed the family's Jewishness that her grandfather and father had rejected. Her happiest moments, she said, "are when I am in the East End amidst Jewish workpeople." A talented linguist, drama teacher and recruiter for trade unionism, she learned Yiddish, avidly read *Fraye Velt*, a radical Yiddish newspaper, and taught adult education classes at a workers' club in Whitechapel established by Yiddish-speaking revolutionaries.

In 1890, when she was invited to address a large indoor rally protesting against the persecution of Jews in Russia, she wrote to the organisers: "I shall be very glad to speak… the more glad that my father was a Jew." She was living in Jews Walk, Sydenham when she committed suicide aged 42. Eleanor had told her sister, "I am Jewishly proud of my house on Jews Walk."

In the 20th century, two organisations provided a sustained Jewish engagement with Karl Marx's ideas. The Arbeter Ring (Workers' Circle) was a Friendly Society, founded in 1909 by Yiddish-speaking Bundists and anarchists, later joined by communists and left-wing Zionists. Its membership peaked in the 1930s. It closed in 1984. Circle members had sharp polemics with each other but all shared Marx's basic philosophical outlook.

The other organisation was the Communist Party, established nationally in Britain three years after the Russian Revolution. In Jewish working-class enclaves in Manchester, London, Leeds and Glasgow in the 1930s, Young Communist League branches were brimming with idealistic Jews, proud that so many Jews sat on the Central Committee of the Bolsheviks who made revolution in Russia.

In 1933, on the 50th anniversary of Marx's death in the city where he had spent the largest portion of his life, a memorial committee purchased a building in Clerkenwell Green and set up a Workers' Library and Trade Union school. The Marx Memorial Library boasts a hall downstairs called the Simcha Hall. Upstairs the bookshelves bear tags honouring book donors, many of them with Jewish names.

Between 1934–37, the Communist Party (CP) doubled its membership nationally, but its largely Jewish East End branches increased fivefold. The Communist Party led militant opposition to Mosley's fascists in that period. When Oswald Mosley told a 15,000-strong rally at Olympia that the principal enemies of fascism were followers of "the German Jew Karl Marx", he was telling the truth for once.

Some historians dismiss Jewish involvement with communism as a brief flirtation reflecting the convergence of Jewish and communist opposition to fascism. Yet, conversation I have had with Jews who joined the Party in that period, even those who later left feeling bitter and betrayed, revealed a deep identification with the Party's Marxist beliefs. Jews whose school lives were cut short by poverty told me how they expanded their education by devouring the Marxist political literature the Party encouraged them to read.

Several of my Jewish teenage friends had erstwhile communist relatives. One friend's father, Ken, had replaced his youthful attachment to communist internationalism with Jewish nationalism – Zionism – and joined the Jewish Male Voice Choir. He visited America, which Party comrades described as an Evil Capitalist Empire, but he came away impressed. Ken did not move far, though, from his working-class roots. He urged me to read *Man's Worldly Goods* – the bible of economics that the Party had introduced him to as a youngster, written by Leo Huberman, an American-Jewish Marxist.

The classic representation of that period in Jewish working-class life, when many Jews felt that affinity with a party that embodied Marx's ideals, was written in the late 1950s by Arnold Wesker. His play, *Chicken Soup with Barley*, centred on a Jewish communist East End family. Scene one begins on the day of the Battle of Cable Street. The family are confident they will see off Mosley, fascism will recede and communism will advance. Sarah, the play's matriarch, is ready to deal Mosley a blow personally with her wooden mixing spoon. By the final scene, set in 1956, both the family and their ideals are disintegrating. Soviet tanks are quelling a popular rising in Hungary. Sarah's son Ronnie urges his mother to open her eyes. But Sarah defends the ideals that brought her into the Party and turns angrily on him: "You want me to give it up now? You want me to move to Hendon and forget who I am?"

That last sentence illustrated the sharpening divide between East End working-class Jews, many influenced by Marx, certain of the place of Jews in the collective struggle for a better world, and those rushing to the suburbs, happy to swap Marx for bourgeois comforts and individualism.

As the Jewish exodus to the suburbs accelerated in the 1960s and 70s, Marx was largely cast aside by those enjoying new prosperity. Their children would be the first in their families to go to university, rather than serve apprenticeships, drive cabs, work the markets or become secretaries. Ironically, in the universities, some of their offspring would encounter Jews for whom Marx remained pivotal.

I was taught by the political theorist Ralph Miliband, who fled to Britain from Nazi-occupied Belgium, Lou Kushnick, a radical Brooklyn-born scholar of race and class in American politics, and the Marxist sociologist Zygmunt Bauman, exiled from his native Poland in 1968 with many other Jews, when antisemitism was weaponised in a bitter power struggle within the Communist Party.

British universities boasted outstanding Jewish proponents of Marx's thinking such as the North American philosophers David-Hillel Ruben and Gerry Cohen, the political scholar Norman Geras and historians Eric Hobsbawm and Raphael Samuel. Samuel's communist aunt Miriam was married to the Jewish Studies professor, Chimen Abramsky, whose personal library included books with Marx's own handwriting in the margins. The New Left of the 1960s and 70s included many suburban Jewish students whose parents were moving rapidly in the opposite political direction.

Jewish scholars talk of *lomedvovniks* – righteous fighters for social justice who appear in each generation. Rabbi Bayfield had his line of prophets. The Polish-Jewish Marxist Isaac Deutscher, who died in London in 1967, identified common traits among the most radical Jewish thinkers.

"Spinoza, Heine, Marx, Rosa Luxemburg, Trotsky… all found Jewry too narrow, too archaic, and too constricting. They all looked for ideals and fulfilment beyond it… yet I think in some ways they were very Jewish indeed… as Jews they dwelt on the borderlines of various civilisations, religions and national cultures… they lived on the margins or in the nooks and crannies of their respective nations… in society and yet not in it, of it and yet not of it. It was this that enabled them to rise in thought above their societies… to strike out mentally into wide new horizons."

Marx is long dead. For most British Jews the struggle against poverty has receded. Jewish institutions have a decidedly conservative face. And yet new Jewish radical movements are springing up today, proving that a bond between part of Anglo-Jewry and Marx's revolutionary ideas continues to renew itself.

Student protests, 1968, journalist George Garrigues documented this graffiti in a university classroom during the socialist and student protests across Europe that year.

"Last night I dreamed a deadly dream, Beyond the Isle of Skye, I saw a dead man win a fight, And I think that man was I."

The Man Who Never Was, opening voiceover

Biographies I – M

Ewen Montagu's book *The Man Who Never Was* formed the basis for the 1956 British film of the same name. It tells the story of a 1943 British Intelligence plan to deceive the Axis powers into thinking the Allied invasion of Sicily would take place elsewhere in the Mediterranean by placing false papers on the body of a tramp dressed as an officer of the Royal Marines.

Louis Jacobs

Rabbi and founder of the
UK Masorti movement
1920–2006

Louis Jacobs was born in
Cheetham, Manchester. His
parents were Harris Jacobs, a
tailor, and Lena née Myerstone.
He was educated at Manchester
Central High School and the
Manchester yeshiva, a college for intensive Torah and Talmudic
education. He received ordination from Rabbi Moshe Segal, head of
the yeshiva, in 1943. In 1945 Jacobs was appointed to the post of
assistant to Dr Munk at his north London synagogue. He enrolled at
University College London to read for a BA honours degree. Jacobs was
appointed Rabbi of Manchester Central Synagogue in 1948. He was
awarded his doctorate on economic life in Talmudic Babylon in 1952. In
1954 he became minister at the New West End Synagogue in London.
He published the controversial *We Have Reason To Believe* in 1957,
questioning the divine origins of the Torah. Jacobs took up a post as
moral tutor at Jews' College. In 1961, when his promotion to principal
was blocked by Chief Rabbi Brodie, he resigned. Brodie used Jacobs'
book to justify his decision, and a furore that came to be known as the
'Jacobs Affair' ensued. In 1962 Jacobs' supporters founded the Society
for the Study of Jewish Theology, to give Jacobs a platform to air his
view that the Torah, although divine, was not the literal word of God
as dictated to Moses. In 1991 the Assembly of Masorti Synagogues
was formed, a movement that shared Jacobs' traditional but non-
fundamentalist theology, and considered him their spiritual leader.

Sydney Jacobson

Journalist, editor and
political commentator
1908–1988

Born in the Transvaal, South
Africa to parents who had
come from Germany, Sydney
Jacobson's first schooling
was in an internment camp
when the family were caught
visiting Germany as the First World War broke out. His father
drowned returning to South Africa when his ship sank. After his
father's death his mother brought him to family in Wales and
then to London. He was educated at the Strand School and
studied journalism at King's College London. He started his career
on the *Daily Express* and then worked for ten years in India on
the *Calcutta Statesman*. On returning to Britain, subsequent jobs
included assistant editor of the magazine *Lilliput*, feature writer for
the *Picture Post* and for the *Sunday Pictorial* (now the *Sunday Mirror*),
political editor of the *Daily Mirror*, editor of the *Daily Herald* and
then the *Sun* and editorial director and deputy chairman of the
Mirror Group. A Labour Party supporter, he produced two famous
front pages supporting the party during the two elections of 1974.
Jacobson was awarded the Military Cross in the Second World War
and in 1975 was made a life peer. Jacobson described himself as
"a non-professing" Jew and was a lifelong Zionist.

Marie Jahoda
Probed the psychology of
unemployment and antisemitism
1907–2001

Marie Jahoda was born in Vienna
to an establishment, secular
Jewish family. After gaining a
PhD at the University of Vienna,
in 1933 she published *Marienthal:
The Sociography of an Unemployed
Community*, which established her reputation as a pioneer in empirical
social research. In 1936, Jahoda was imprisoned for her affiliation
with the Social Revolutionaries, and released after seven months on
condition that she left the country. She fled to London, and worked
as an assistant editor at the *Wartime Social Survey*. After the war,
Jahoda moved to the USA and worked in the department of scientific
research of the American Jewish Committee. In 1949 she became
Professor of Social Psychology and Director of the Research Centre
for Human Relations at New York University. She became the first
female president of the Society for the Psychological Study of
Social Issues in 1953. Returning to England in 1958 to marry Labour
MP Austen Harry Albu, she became Senior Lecturer in Psychology
at Brunel College of Advanced Technology. In 1962 she became
Professor of Psychology there. In 1965, Jahoda set up the UK's first
department of social psychology, at the new University of Sussex.
She was awarded a CBE in 1974.

Immanuel Jakobovits
Chief Rabbi
1921–1999

Immanuel Jakobovits was born in Konigsberg, East Prussia, Germany and grew up in Berlin. He emigrated to England from Nazi Germany in 1936. He attended Etz Chaim Yeshiva, Jews' College Theological Seminary and London University, receiving a rabbinical diploma and a PhD. Immanuel served as a minister of the London synagogues of Brondesbury, South East London and the Great. In 1949 he became Chief Rabbi of Ireland and in 1958 minister of the Fifth Avenue Synagogue in New York. In 1966 he was appointed Chief Rabbi of the United Hebrew Congregations of the British Commonwealth and became the leading spokesman for British Jews and an acknowledged moral leader. He was the first chief rabbi to be knighted (1981) and the first to become a peer and sit in the House of Lords (1988). He developed Jewish education, establishing a network of schools. He published Jewish Medical Ethics and the media frequently asked him to speak on issues such as *in vitro* fertilisation or transplant surgery. Jakobovits was a voice for family values and individual responsibility and was much admired by Margaret Thatcher. He was a supporter of Israel but also criticised Israeli government policies. Family holidays were always in a caravan and Jakobovits was President of the Caravanning Club.

Lisa Jardine

Historian, academic and
intellectual with populist appeal
1944–2015

Lisa Jardine was born in
Oxford, the daughter of
scientist and broadcaster Jacob
Bronowski, who was a refugee
from Poland. Jardine saw no
distinction between literature
and science and applied her scholarship to a range of subjects from
comprehensive education to a historical analysis of the Renaissance.
She had a talent for making academic debates entertaining as well
as informative. The first woman fellow of Jesus College, Cambridge
(1976–89), she always drew attention to female influences on
national, literary and scientific events. A keen biographer, she
created the Centre for Editing Lives and Letters (CELL) in 2002
when she moved to Queen Mary University, London. She wrote many
bestsellers, including a biography of Sir Christopher Wren (2002)
and *Ingenious Pursuits: Building the Scientific Revolution* (1999). A
passionate believer in the value of experimental science and the need
for regulation, Jardine became chair of the Human Fertilisation and
Embryology Authority (2006–12). She was chair of judges for the
Booker Prize (2002), trustee of the Victoria and Albert Museum,
appointed CBE (2005) and made a fellow of the Royal Society
(2015). Jardine maintained that her Jewish heritage gave her a cultural
richness and a classlessness that allowed her the freedom to choose
to belong or not.

Nathan S. Joseph
Architect and social worker
1834–1909

Nathan Solomon Joseph was born in the Minories, London. He was one of nine children of Solomon Joseph, a City merchant, and his wife Jane Selig. Joseph was educated by private tutors at home before enrolling at University College London, where he graduated with the civil engineering prize. On graduation he turned to architecture and became the foremost in the first wave of great Anglo-Jewish architects that included Edward Salomons and Hyman Henry Collins. He was brother-in-law to Chief Rabbi Hermann Adler, a relationship that greatly facilitated his career during the golden age of the "cathedral synagogue" in Britain. Added to his considerable architectural achievements, Joseph had a great social conscience and campaigned for social housing, free seats in the synagogue for poor Jews and educational buildings. He was active in the Jewish Board of Guardians and a founder member of the Russo-Jewish Committee, established in 1882 in response to the pogroms in eastern Europe. He was also the Honorary Secretary of Jews' College and founded the Jewish Religious Union in 1902, which evolved into the Liberal Synagogue shortly after his death.

Tony Judt

He wrote incisive analyses
of international politics
1948–2010

Tony Judt was born in Hackney,
London to parents who had fled
eastern Europe. The family was
secular but with a strong political
and cultural affiliation to Judaism.
Judt was a passionate left-wing
Zionist until he travelled to Israel in 1967 and became disillusioned
by Israel's nationalism and anti-Arab stance. The experience gave
Judt a lifelong distrust of political and religious dogma and in later
life he described himself as a "universalist social democrat". Nothing
escaped Judt's brilliant intellectual scrutiny. His academic subject was
19th-century French socialism but he was quick to criticise left-wing
French intellectuals who continued to support Soviet Marxism even
when confronted with the horrors perpetuated by the Russian state.
Judt settled in America and loved the country's energy and openness
but rejected its lack of social democracy and, particularly after 9/11,
distrusted its foreign policy. His greatest work in 2005 was *Post-war:
a History of Europe since 1945*. Judt was diagnosed with a form of
motor neurone disease in 2008. Near the end of his life he wrote
an article for the *New York Review of Books* criticising Israel's religious
fervour and refusal to cooperate with the Palestinians. The article
resulted in cancelled lectures and a huge backlash.

Richard Kahn

Economist who pioneered
work on the multiplier
1905–1989

Richard Kahn was born in
Hampstead, London and raised
in an Orthodox Jewish family.
Kahn attended St Paul's School
before reading mathematics and
then physics at Cambridge. His
schooling in economics came from Gerald Shove and John Maynard
Keynes, who helped him achieve a first in 1928. He became a fellow
of King's College two years later and would go on to spend the
majority of his career there. Following the publication of Keynes's *A
Treatise on Money* (1930), Kahn was invited to join the Cambridge
Circus discussion group with four other Cambridge economists. Their
feedback was influential in the writing of Keynes's *General Theory*,
published in 1936. Kahn became a professor of economics in 1951
and Bursar of King's College, taking over the post from Keynes. His
most significant achievement in the field was outlined in his 1931
article, "The Relation of Home Investment to Unemployment". In this
piece he put forward his concept of the multiplier, a way of measuring
the effect of increasing aggregate expenditure on net national
product. Kahn was later an outspoken critic of Margaret Thatcher's
monetarist policies. He was appointed CBE in 1946 and became
Baron Kahn of Hampstead in 1965.

Nicholas Kaldor

Adviser on social reform projects
1908–1986

Nicholas Kaldor was born in Budapest, Hungary. His father was a Jewish lawyer. Kaldor studied at the Minta Gymnasium in Budapest and the University of Berlin, then read for his honours degree in economics at the London School of Economics. Two years later he joined the economics department at the LSE, becoming a reader in 1945 and an honorary fellow in 1970. While there he made numerous research breakthroughs, notably in the field of capital theory and welfare economics. Kaldor joined King's College, Cambridge in 1949 and became a professor in 1966. He was instrumental in the establishment of the "Cambridge School", which expanded on the ideas of his friend John Maynard Keynes. Outside of the academic sphere, Kaldor worked in a number of advisory positions. He assisted the social reformer Lord Beveridge with his reports during the Second World War, including *Full Employment in a Free Society* (1944). He was also invited to advise on taxation by several developing countries. Kaldor became a special adviser to the Labour government in 1964, and was made a life peer in 1974. Baron Kaldor embraced English history and culture and strongly opposed Conservative economic policy under Margaret Thatcher.

A HISTORICAL AND
CRITICAL COMMENTARY
ON THE OLD TESTAMENT
: WITH A NEW
TRANSLATION, LEVITICUS
VOLUME 1   Volume 1

KALISCH, MARCUS MORITZ, 1828-1885

Marcus Kalisch

Prolific Biblical commentator
and writer

1828–1885

Marcus Kalisch was a respected writer and biblical commentator. He was born in Pomerania and later studied at the University of Berlin. There he contributed to the struggle to bring democracy to Germany but left disappointed. In 1848 he moved to England, where he was appointed Secretary to the Chief Rabbi, Dr Nathan Marcus Adler. Kalisch also worked as a tutor for the Rothschild family. He is best known for his *Historical and Critical Commentary on the Old Testament*, which brought together all existing analyses of the Bible's various books. His third volume in the series, *Leviticus*, was considered groundbreaking. Kalisch argued that the priestly rituals described within the book actually reflected practices from the period *after* the Jews were exiled from the Holy Land. This showed that the work must have been written in several stages. This commentary was well received and influenced later scholars such as Julius Wellhausen. Kalisch also authored a Hebrew grammar book and a work entitled *Path and Goal: A Discussion on the Elements of Civilisation and the Conditions of Happiness*, which illustrated the many views of human destiny found in different religious traditions. Although Kalisch wrote about many different religious systems, he remained committed to his Jewish faith.

Casriel Dovid Kaplin
Rabbi and scholar
1931–2006

Casriel Dovid Kaplin was born in the East End of London. His father was Jerusalem-born Noach Kaplin. The Kaplin family was evacuated to Letchworth in Hertfordshire during the Second World War to escape the heavy bombing in the London Docklands. Kaplin had his barmitzvah while living in Letchworth. After the war he studied at the Gateshead yeshiva. Kaplin transferred to the Chevron yeshiva in 1952 before returning to Gateshead at which time he was accepted in Gateshead kollel. There he received semicha, a qualification whereby a Jewish man can become a rabbi, from, among others, Rabbi Tzvi Pesach Frank, renowned halachic scholar and Chief Rabbi of Jerusalem. In 1965 he was appointed rabbi of the Shomrei Hadath Synagogue in Hampstead, London. He transferred to the London Beth Din and remained in post there for 30 years. His reputation grew throughout his life and he began to receive rabbinical questions from all over the world. In 1988 he retired to Israel, where he was invited to serve as rosh kollel of the Yeshivas Toras Chochom.

Elie Kedourie
Challenged contemporary
views on the Middle East
1926–1992

Elie Kedourie grew up in Baghdad
and came to England to take his
undergraduate degree at the
London School of Economics.
He made a lifelong study of
the Middle East and, contrary
to the prevailing wisdom of the time, he argued in favour of British
and French domination and against nationalism and independence.
These dissenting views were deeply unpopular and in 1953 Kedourie
withdrew his thesis due to his Oxford examiner, Sir Hamilton Gibb,
deeming the polemic abhorrent. Kedourie was Lecturer in Politics at
the London School of Economics from 1953 until 1990. There he
warned against British withdrawal from the Arab States, which he said
would open the way to local despots. He believed that Britain had a
civilising role and that leaving the Middle East constituted diplomatic
failure. His most famous book, *Nationalism* (1960), was a denunciation
of the idea that self-determination was either a worthy political aim
or part of a long historical tradition. His conservative views brought
him into conflict with another respected historian, Arnold Toynbee.
Kedourie became disillusioned with the expansion of universities and
what he saw as falling standards. He was lecturing in America when he
died of heart failure. An observant Jew, he published *The Jewish World*
in 1986, a discourse on what constitutes Jewishness.

Michael Kidron

Radical thinker
and cartographer
1930–2003

Michael Kidron was born in Cape Town, South Africa. His family were passionate Zionists but he rejected the movement soon after joining them in Palestine while studying at Tichon Hadash in Tel Aviv. Kidron read economics at the Hebrew University of Jerusalem before leaving Israel for Balliol College, Oxford. There his libertarian Marxism flourished as he rejected the authoritarian approach of others in the communist movement. These ideas found support in the Socialist Review Group, where he joined his brother-in-law Tony Cliff in criticising the Soviet bloc and instead championing the capitalist working class. Kidron's belief was that in order to change the world one needed to understand how it worked in reality instead of proposing ideological alternatives. He directed his research to capitalism, publishing *Western Capitalism Since the War* (1968), which developed the concept of the permanent arms economy. His version of left-wing ideology was marked by honesty rather than dogma, and this was exemplified in the *International Socialism* journals he edited. Kidron's internationalism was rendered most vividly in the *State of the World Atlas*, which he co-authored in 1981 and the *War Atlas* in 1983.

Melanie Klein
Psychoanalyst
1882–1960

Melanie Reizes was born in Vienna. Her father was Moritz Reizes, a doctor and dentist, and her mother was Libussa Deutsch, the granddaughter of a liberal rabbi. At 21 she married Arthur S. Klein, an engineer, whose work involved frequent moves around Europe. In 1914 Klein found herself in Prague, where, struggling with the death of her mother, she entered analysis with Sandor Ferenczi, an early follower of Freud. By 1919 Klein had begun to make her own observations in children, based on her daughter and two sons. In 1921 she wrote her first paper "The development of a child". Klein was one of the first psychoanalysts to confirm Freud's theories of child development – which he had formulated from his work with adults – by observing children. Klein's breakthrough was to use the child's natural means of expression – play. She gave her subjects a set of toys each and observed their interactions during the third year of life. Klein was invited to London by Alix Strachey, wife of Freud's translator James Strachey, and settled in St John's Wood. She became a leading figure in the British Psychoanalytical Society, but found herself in opposition to the methods and findings of another leading child psychotherapist, Anna Freud, resulting in an institutional opposition between the Vienna Psychoanalytical Society and the British. Klein published her major work *The Psychoanalysis of Children* in 1932. A definitive collection of all her published work, *The Writings of Melanie Klein*, appeared in 1975. Her play technique remains a standard method of child psychotherapists.

"The highly ambitious person, in spite of all his successes, always remains dissatisfied, in the same way as a greedy baby is never satisfied."
Melanie Klein

Ludwig Koch

He brought the sounds of the
countryside to radio listeners
1881 – 1974

Born in Frankfurt, the son
of German Jews, Ludwig
Koch was given an Edison
phonograph as a child and
began recording the sounds
of his numerous pets. Koch
was also a child violinist and member of Clara Schumann's music
circle. His career as a concert singer was cut short by the outbreak
of the First World War when he joined the military intelligence. In
1928, while employed by the German subsidiary of Electric and
Musical Industries (EMI), Koch began recording animal sounds and
developed the idea of a sound-book, a gramophone record that
could be sold to accompany an illustrated book. In 1936 Koch fled
the Nazis and moved to London, where he collaborated with E. M.
(Max) Nicholson on the sound-book *Songs of Wild Birds* (1936),
which was followed by *More Songs of Wild Birds* in 1937. Koch became
a well-known voice on BBC radio and used his recordings to illustrate
his *Children's Hour* talks. He played a part in the early days of the
Bristol-based natural history programmes unit of the BBC and sold
them his entire collection of animal recordings. The collection is now
housed in the National Sound Archive at the British Library. Koch
was appointed MBE in 1960.

Otto Kurz

Art historian specialising in
Middle Eastern and Baroque art
1908–1975

A secular Jew born in Vienna,
Austria, Kurz studied art
history at the University of
Vienna. He collaborated with
Ernst Kris on *Legend, Myth and
Magic in the Image of the Artist*
(1934) and *Fakes: A Handbook for Collectors and Students* (1948). In
1933 Kurz was beaten up on campus by Nazi thugs. As he was no
longer able to work in Austria, Kurz's tutor Julius von Schlosser found
him a job at the library of the Warburg Institute in Hamburg. When
the institute moved to London, Kurz was invited to follow and became
head librarian in 1949. He took up the post of Professor of History of
Classical Tradition at the University of London in 1965 and was made
Professor of Fine Art first at the Slade and then at the University of
Oxford (1970–1), where his subject was Islamic art between east and
west. In 1943 Kurz was commissioned by Anthony Blunt to catalogue
the collection of Bolognese drawings at Windsor Castle (published
1955). He was a visiting lecturer at the Hebrew University (1964,
1973) and fellow of the British Academy. Kurz never forgot his debt
to Julius von Schlosser and wrote his mentor's memoir in 1955.

Stephan Körner

Strove to make philosophical concepts accessible to all

1913–2000

Stephan Körner was a Czech-born philosopher who fled his native land when the Nazis invaded in 1938. He travelled through Poland, arriving in England as a refugee at the outbreak of the Second World War. Körner studied at Cambridge under the celebrated philosopher Wittgenstein and provided for himself by serving as a waiter in a Greek restaurant. During his professorship at the University of Bristol, Körner published his two most famous works: *Kant* served as a general introduction to the German philosopher's tricky concepts while *Conceptual Thinking* dealt with Körner's belief in exact and inexact concepts. He argued that exact concepts, such as mathematical ideas, can be clearly defined, whereas inexact concepts, such as the perception of colour, are related to sense experience and have unclear boundaries. Although Körner managed to escape the Nazis, his parents both died in the Holocaust. His first cousin, Ruth Maier, died at Auschwitz and became known as Norway's Anne Frank after her wartime diaries were discovered. Stephan was devoted to his wife Edith (a magistrate and NHS reformer) and the pair committed suicide after Edith was diagnosed with terminal cancer. Their son is the mathematician Thomas Körner.

Imre Lakatos

From Hungarian official
to British academic
1922–1974

Born Imre Lipsitz to wine
merchant Jacob Lipsitz and his
wife Margit, Lakatos changed his
name in order to sound more
working-class, in line with his
communist ideals. Lakatos came to
Britain in 1956 and, after completing a second PhD at Cambridge, was
appointed to a lectureship in logic and the philosophy of mathematics
at the London School of Economics. His major work *Proofs and
Refutations* was a detailed examination of the relationship between the
number of edges, faces and vertices of polyhedrons. Before his long
career in academia, Lakatos was a high-ranking official in the Hungarian
government. However, he later fell foul of the communist authorities.
During the Second World War, Lakatos was given shelter by some non-
Jews in Romania; he was joined by other Jews including one Eva Izsak.
There is speculation that her whereabouts was known to the Gestapo,
and she therefore jeopardised the safety of the entire group. Lakatos
proposed that she be coerced into committing suicide in a nearby
town to divert attention from the rest of the cell. Izsak poisoned
herself in some woods outside Debrecan and her body was found
by a child. This wartime affair came to light in the early 1950s and
Lakatos' involvement was called into question. He was interned
in a labour camp for three years. His communist connections were
never forgotten and the British government were distrustful, denying
him naturalisation.

Sidney Lee

Lifelong scholar and
Shakespeare enthusiast
1859–1926

Sidney Lee was born Solomon
Lazarus Lee in Bloomsbury,
London, the elder son of Lazarus
Lee and his wife, Jessie Davis.
Although of Jewish descent, he
was not in adult life a practising
Jew. He was educated at the City of London School, and went on to
read modern history at Balliol College, Oxford, graduating in 1882.
During his time as an undergraduate, he contributed two articles
on Shakespeare to the *Gentleman's Magazine*. The adoption of the
name "Sidney" instead of "Solomon" after 1890 was reputedly due
to the advice of Benjamin Jowett, master of his college. In 1883, Lee
became Assistant Editor of the *Dictionary of National Biography*, and
succeeded Sir Leslie Stephen as editor in 1891. Despite his taxing
work for the *Dictionary*, he also maintained his Shakespearean work,
and in 1898 published *The Life of William Shakespeare*. In 1902, he
edited the Oxford facsimile edition of the First Folio of Shakespeare's
comedies, histories and tragedies, followed by the complete
edition of Shakespeare's works in 1906. Lee was knighted in 1911.
From 1913 to 1924 he served as Professor of English Literature and
Language at Queen Mary University, London. His other notable
works include *A Life of Queen Victoria* (1902), *Great Englishmen of the
Sixteenth Century* (1904), *Shakespeare and the Modern Stage* (1906)
and *King Edward VII, a Biography* (1925).

Joseph Leftwich

Introduced Yiddish literature
to the English-speaking world
1892–1983

Born in Holland, Joseph
Lefkowitz, the son of a Polish-
Jewish cobbler, moved to London
at the age of five. In his own
words, he became an "English
schoolboy at a Whitechapel
board school" where he was known as "Lefty". His formal education
ended when he was 14, but through private studies, he widened his
knowledge of English and Yiddish literature. He was a member of
the "Whitechapel Boys" group of aspiring young Jewish writers in
London's East End from 1910–1914, a name that he coined himself.
He also worked as a furrier, a tailor and a baker before becoming
the editor of the London branch of the Jewish Telegraphic Agency
in 1921. The rise of the Nazis compelled him to write *What Will
Happen to the Jews?* (1936). Post-war he published *The Tragedy of
Anti-Semitism* (1948), and from 1945 he served as Director of the
British Federation of Jewish Relief Organizations until his late 80s.
Leftwich became well-known for his Yiddish literature, translating and
editing two influential anthologies of poetry: *Yisröel, the First Jewish
Omnibus* (1933) and *The Golden Peacock* (1939). He published a new
anthology of Yiddish essays in English translation, *The Way We Think*,
in 1969. For more than 40 years, he was the permanent delegate of
the Yiddish PEN Club centre in New York and on the executive of
PEN, the world organisation of writers, where he protested against
the purge of Yiddish writers in the Soviet Union.

Gottlieb Wilhelm Leitner

Educationist, orientalist
and polyglot
1840–1899

Born Gottlieb Wilhelm Sapier in Hungary, and educated in Constantinople, Leitner later took his stepfather's name. From an early age, he had a precocious aptitude for languages. At 15 he became a first-class interpreter to the British Commissariat at Constantinople and was awarded the rank of Honorary Colonel. In 1858 he moved to London to study at King's College. Two years later he was appointed Professor of Arabic and Mohammedan Law. In 1862 he was naturalised as a British subject. In 1869 he studied law at the Middle Temple, and in 1875 was called to the bar. In 1864 Leitner became Principal of the Government College at Lahore, India, where he remained for 15 years. There he founded many schools, learning programmes and publications, including the *Civil and Military Gazette*. In 1877 Leitner published *Results of a Tour in Dardistan* recounting his expedition to an unexplored region of the Kurdish mountains. His knowledge of Indian customs and culture led him to suggest that Queen Victoria style herself 'kaisar-i-Hind' (Empress of India) which became the Queen's accepted title. Leitner's admiration for Indian culture and determination to treat Indians as social and intellectual equals was unusual at the time. In 1883 he established the Oriental Institute in Woking, a building that incorporated the first mosque to be built in Britain. Leitner identified as an Anglican, although his Jewish origins were widely known, and a notice of his death was published in the *Jewish Chronicle*.

David Levi

Defender of the Jewish faith
1742–1801

David Levi, the son of Polish immigrants, was born into poverty in London. His grandfather tutored him in Hebrew. David became a shoemaker, hatter and printer and he remained dedicated to his religion, studying Hebrew works and Jewish literature in his spare time. Levi became concerned that Enlightenment thinkers such as Voltaire, Hume and Spinoza were having a detrimental effect upon his beloved Jewish community, as scientific discoveries were calling older religious philosophies into question. In order to revive interest in Jewish tradition, he independently published introductory works to Jewish rituals and refutations of Christian misconceptions about the Jews. His most famous book, published in 1782, was entitled *A Succinct Account of the Rites and Ceremonies of the Jews*. Levi also published translations of the prayer books of both the Ashkenazi and Sephardi communities. Levi strongly argued against forced conversion to Christianity and warned against the Christian millennial idea that Judgement Day was near and would bring punishment of Jews who failed to convert. David Levi was an active member of his synagogue's congregation and wrote short poems that were frequently read at services.

Bernard Levin
A journalist with a punch
1928–2004

Bernard Levin was born in London and was brought up by his maternal grandparents, who were immigrants from Lithuania. It was not a religious household, but his mother would mark the holy days. In 1953 he was appointed to *Truth* magazine. The editor George Scott allegedly gave Levin the job after hearing his surname, and believed that by appointing a Jew he could change the magazine's reputation for being right-wing. Later Levin joined the *Spectator*, emerging as a brilliant polemicist who divided politicians into either good or bad, with no in-between. Levin also worked as theatre critic alongside Robert Muller. The two became known as "the kosher butchers" for their tough reviews. Levin appeared on the BBC's *That Was the Week That Was*, where he was famously punched by an audience member who was angry about a harsh review that Levin had written about his actress wife. Levin enjoyed a 26-year career at *The Times* and calculated in 1998 that he had written over 17m words. He felt alienated from his Jewish heritage and joined the Movement for Spiritual Awareness. He maintained that he felt closer to the teachings of Buddhism and Christianity than Judaism.

Hirschel Levin

Rabbi and scholar

1721–1800

Hirschel Ben Arye Lob Levin was born in Rzeszow, in the Polish Lithuanian Commonwealth. His father Saul Levin was a rabbi in Amsterdam, and his mother was the daughter of Rabbi Chacham Zvi Ashkenazi. He formed a reputation as a scholarly Talmudist. In 1751, at the age of just 30, he weighed in on the doctrinal struggle between Jacob Emden and Jonathan Eybeschutz, coming down firmly on the side of Emden, who was his uncle on his mother's side. In 1756, he was elected Chief Rabbi of the London congregation of German and Polish Jews. In 1760 Levin became embroiled in a disagreement when he defended London's community of Jewish butchers against criticism from Jacob Kimhi. When his synagogue denied him permission to respond publicly he resigned, accepting the position of rabbi of Halberstadt in 1763. He went on to become rabbi of Mannheim and, in 1772, of Berlin. Levin was a great friend of the composer Felix Mendelssohn. Levin's son, Rabbi Solomon Hirschell, was also Chief Rabbi, the first of the British Empire.

Geoffrey Lewis
Linguist
1920–2008

Geoffrey Lewis was born in Hackney, London. His father was Ashley Lewis, a factory foreman, and his mother was Jeanne Muriel née Cohen Sintrop. He was educated at University College School in London and then went on to St John's College, Oxford, to read Classics. He graduated in 1940, then joined the Royal Air Force. He served for five years, mostly as a radar operator in Libya and Egypt. It was there that he taught himself Turkish. In 1945 Lewis returned to Britain with his heart set on an academic career. He enrolled on a second BA course in Arabic and Persian, which he completed in 1947. He was awarded the James Mew Scholarship to fund his doctoral studies, but before embarking on his research he spent six months in Turkey immersing himself in the language and culture. He completed his DPhil in 1950. In the same year he became the first Lecturer in Turkish at the University of Oxford. In 1954 he became Senior Lecturer in Islamic Studies, and ten years later took up the new post of Senior Lecturer in Turkish. A Turkish chair was created for him in 1986. From 1987 he was an emeritus professor of St Anthony's College, Oxford. Lewis wrote widely on his subject and from "how to" books such as *Teach Yourself Turkish* (1953) to more academic works such as *Albucasis on Surgery and Instruments* (1973). He worked tirelessly to enhance Turco-British relations, and he was honoured for his work by both countries. In 1998 he was made a CMG in Britain and awarded Turkey's Order of Merit.

David Malcolm Lewis

Classical scholar and international authority on Greek history

1928–1994

David Malcolm Lewis was born in Willesden, London. His parents were second-generation immigrants from Poland and Lithuania. Lewis was an undergraduate at Oxford University and studied for his PhD at Princeton University. He also spent time at the Institute for Advanced Study at Princeton, which he called the "Mecca of Greek epigraphy". At the British School in Athens he worked on his specialism epigraphy, the interpretation of Greek inscriptions on stone. He later returned to Oxford University as Professor of Ancient History, and remained there for most of his professional life. His scholarship included becoming a linguist of ancient languages and collecting coins of the period as well as studying Middle Eastern history. He wrote *Sparta and Persia* (1977) and always aimed to produce an imaginative recreation of ancient history to give it a wider relevance. Between 1977 and 1994 he was involved with producing the new edition of the *Cambridge Ancient History*. A great scholar, collaborator, editor and a generous teacher, he was willing to assist others drafting articles, theses and books. Lewis had a strong Jewish faith and was an active member of the Oxford Hebrew congregation when a new synagogue was built on Nelson Street in the suburb known as Jericho. In 1992 Lewis wrote a cultural, religious and historical study entitled *The Jews of Oxford*.

Jacob of London
First *Presbyter Judaeorum*
fl. 1199–1217

Jacob of London was appointed by King John as first *Presbyter Judaeorum* in 1199. The king also gave him a safe conduct, no small thing in the atmosphere of violent antisemitism that prevailed in England at the time. In 1198 Pope Innocent III wrote to all Christian princes demanding the remission of usury demanded by Jews from Christians, an edict that would make their existence impossible. King John, however, treated the Jewish community with forbearance, due to the fact that he had become indebted to them while in Ireland, and created the position of chief official of the Jews of England for Jacob. Jacob is possibly the rabbi Jacob of London who translated the entire Haggadah, a Jewish text that sets forth the order of the Passover Seder into the vernacular so that it could be understood by women and children. It is thought that Jacob died in 1217, as Josce of London is mentioned as his successor from that date.

Dennis Lyons
Public relations consultant
1918–1978

Born Braham Jack Lyons in
Brighton, the son of a turf
accountant, he became a
journalist and a public relations
consultant. Lyons was the
main speechwriter for Harold
Wilson, and coined the phrases
"yesterday's men" (1970), the "social contract" (1972) and others
from Wilson's rhetorical armoury. He shrouded much of his career
in secrecy, and was virtually unknown to the public when Wilson
unexpectedly awarded him a life peerage in 1974.

Hyam Maccoby

Controversial Jewish scholar who
challenged Christian beliefs
1924–2004

Born in Sunderland, Maccoby
learned Biblical Hebrew and
Talmudic Aramaic from the age
of four. His grandfather was
a *maggid* (itinerant religious
preacher) in Poland. After
studying at Oxford University and a period in the army at Bletchley,
Maccoby became a librarian and tutor at Leo Baeck College, London,
where Reform and Liberal rabbis trained. Maccoby had a talent for
making ancient history and theology relevant and exciting, although
his views were always controversial. An Orthodox Jew, he portrayed
Jesus as leading the resistance against oppressive Roman rule rather
than opposing Judaism. Furthermore, in his book *The Mythmaker:
Paul and the Invention of Christianity* (1986), Maccoby states that
Jesus had no intention of starting a new religion and berates Paul of
Tarsus for casting him in this light. One of Maccoby's many television
appearances was in Howard Jacobson's documentary *Sorry, Judas*
(1993), inspired by Maccoby's book *Judas Iscariot and the Myth of
Jewish Evil* (1992), which outlined the connection between the New
Testament and Auschwitz. In 1998, Maccoby became a professor
at the Centre for Jewish Studies at Leeds University. Never slow to
tackle prejudice, Maccoby wrote a brilliant analysis of T. S. Eliot's
antisemitic outbursts in 1973.

Philip Magnus
Visionary educationist who
promoted technical education
1842–1933

Born in High Holborn, Magnus
attended University College
London gaining first-class degrees
first in arts and then in science.
An advocate of Jewish reform,
Magnus studied religion in Berlin
and upon his return became a rabbi at the West London Synagogue,
a Reform synagogue near Portland Place, London. He supplemented
his income by tutoring private students in mathematics, mechanics
and physics and then began lecturing and examining for educational
institutions. He returned to his *alma mater* UCL as a lecturer and tried,
unsuccessfully, to reform the University of London from within. In
1880 he was appointed director of the newly created City and Guilds
of London Institute for the Advancement of Technical Education and
remained their principal administrator for 35 years. After becoming
a national figure, the new Liberal government made him a member of
the Royal Commission on Technical Instruction in 1881. Magnus was
awarded a knighthood for his services to education. Between 1906
and 1922 he was a Unionist MP representing London University and
became the first Jew to serve as a representative for a university seat.
In 1917 he accepted a baronetcy. Magnus served as Chairman of the
Jewish War Memorial Council, as a Vice-President of the Jewish Board
of Deputies, the Anglo-Jewish Association and Jews' College. His bestselling textbook, *Lessons in Elementary Mechanics* (1875), was the first of
a long series of elementary science textbooks published by Longmans.

Philip Magnus-Allcroft

He revived interest in
the Victorian era
1906–1988

Philip Magnus-Allcroft was born
in London to Laurie Magnus,
director of Routledge Publishing,
and his wife Dora Spielman.
His grandfather was Sir Philip
Magnus, first Baronet, and
Magnus-Allcroft inherited the title in 1933. The family were notably
active within the Jewish community of London. After graduating
from Wadham College Oxford, Magnus-Allcroft worked for the
Board of Education. During the Second World War he served in the
Royal Artillery and rose to the rank of major. He is best known for a
number of biographies he wrote, beginning with his study of Edmund
Burke (1939). He gained success and national recognition with his
biography of Gladstone (1954), which used new material and revived
a general interest in the Victorian period. Magnus-Allcroft was the
first to reveal Gladstone's rehabilitative work with prostitutes. This
was followed by other books on Kitchener, Sir Walter Raleigh and
King Edward VII. Magnus-Allcroft was also a trustee of the National
Portrait Gallery and an editor of the *Jewish Guardian*.

Karl Mannheim
Sociologist
1893–1947

Karoly Mannheim was born in Budapest, Hungary. His parents were Gustav Mannheim, a textile merchant, and Rosa Eylenburg. Mannheim was educated at a gymnasium, then at the University of Budapest, where he read philosophy. He graduated in 1915 and obtained his doctorate in 1918. He was appointed Lecturer at the College of Education in Budapest, but after a counter-revolutionary government came to power Mannheim left for Vienna in 1919, and from thence went to Germany. Under the Weimar Republic he became part of the intellectual circle around Max and Alfred Weber. Many of his key publications were written in this period, notably *Ideologie und Utopie* (1929). He took up various posts at German universities until the Nazis seized power. He came to England, settling in Golders Green, and took up a lectureship in sociology at the London School of Economics. He became a British citizen in 1940. He lectured on a part-time basis for the University of London Institute of Education from 1941–1945. In 1946 he was given a full-time chair at the institute. At the LSE he had a somewhat strained relationship with his colleagues, especially Professor of Sociology Morris Ginsberg. He became passionately concerned with social reconstruction after the Second World War and wrote widely on the sociology of education and planning for democracy. His *Times* obituary observed that, in common with many other émigré academics, Mannheim had become "more English than the English themselves."

David Margoliouth

Born into Christianity, schooled in Judaism, expert in Islam
1858–1940

David Margoliouth was born in London to parents Ezekiel and Sarah. His father had converted to Anglicanism before David's birth and worked as a missionary to Jews in the city. In 1877 David began his almost 60-year connection with the University of Oxford when he embarked on his studies. While a student he won a host of academic prizes and stayed on as a tutor in classics after graduating. In 1889 he was appointed Laudian Chair of Arabic, despite his application making no mention of any knowledge of the language. However, in his first five years he had published two well-received Arabic studies that served students for many years to come. Margoliouth also wrote a number of works related to Islamic history, including *Mohammed and the Rise of Islam* and *Relations between Arabs and Israelites Prior to the Rise of Islam*. During the First World War Margoliouth lectured in India, Egypt and Iraq, where he came to be considered more knowledgeable than native Islamic scholars. This was despite the fact that he was rather difficult to understand, both in English and Arabic, due to a speech impediment. During his time at Oxford he was ordained as an Anglican minister.

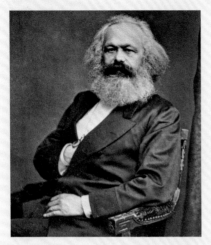

Karl Marx

The father of Communism

1818–1883

Karl Marx was born in Prussia, the third of nine children. His parents, Heinrich and Henriette, were both from rabbinical families. Heinrich was baptised into the Lutheran church at the age of 35, thus breaking with the rest of the Jewish Marx family. The young Marx enjoyed a riotous undergraduate career at the University of Bonn. Exiled for his extreme views, Marx then found work on a radical newspaper in Paris. He embarked on a study of the French Revolution and found a kindred spirit in in Friedrich Engels, who also wrote on the subject. Finding accord with Engels on all matters of political theory, Marx wrote his major work, the *Communist Manifesto (1848)*. Expelled from Belgium following the February Revolution of the same year, Marx became a political exile and in 1850 settled in London. There he lived with his wife Jenny and his growing family in Dickensian squalor in Soho. Beset by money troubles, he described himself as being in a "constant state of siege" from creditors. Having experienced society's inequities at first hand, his *Das Kapital* (1867) set forth a new structure for society, economics and class structure. Baptised as a Lutheran in the wake of his father's conversion, Karl Marx held no discernible loyalty either to Christianity or his Jewish heritage, fostering a distrust of all organised religions as "the opiate of the people."

Stadtplan

DDR 2,00 M

KARL-MARX-STADT

ohne Randgebiete ca 1:15 000

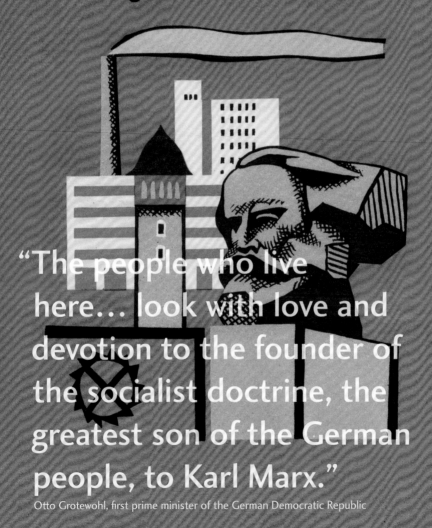

"The people who live here… look with love and devotion to the founder of the socialist doctrine, the greatest son of the German people, to Karl Marx."

Otto Grotewohl, first prime minister of the German Democratic Republic

Albert Meltzer

Revolutionary anarchist
and publisher
1920–1996

Born in Hackney, east London,
Albert Meltzer attended the
Latymer School and became
an anarchist at the age of 15.
During the Spanish Civil War,
Meltzer helped smuggle arms to
the anarcho-syndicalist CNT. At the outbreak of the Second World
War, Meltzer symbolically registered as a conscientious objector
before enlisting. Perhaps because of his politics, Meltzer was not
sent overseas until after the war. When he was finally sent to Egypt
in 1946, he participated in a mutiny that briefly established soldiers'
councils. After the war Meltzer wrote for the long-running anarchist
newspaper *Freedom* but would later denounce the collective for their
broad-church approach to anarchism, which opposed Meltzer's
emphasis on working class self-emancipation. In 1967 Meltzer and
frequent collaborator Stuart Christie founded the prisoner support
group Anarchist Black Cross and in 1970 they began publishing the
periodical *Black Flag*. In 1979 Meltzer also helped found the Kate
Sharpley Library, dedicated to preserving anarchist history. Meltzer
continued to be a familiar and controversial figure in the anarchist
movement until his death in 1996. His writings include *The Floodgates
of Anarchy* (1969, co-authored with Stuart Christie), *Anarchism:
Arguments for and Against* (1981) and the memoir *I Couldn't Paint
Golden Angels* (1996).

Frederick de Sola Mendes

Rabbi and scholar
1850–1927

Frederick de Sola Mendes was born in Montego Bay, Jamaica. He was the son of Abraham Pereira Mendes and Eliza de Sola. His father and grandfather were rabbis. He was educated at Northwick College, University College School and the University of London. He then went to Germany to study rabbinics at the Jewish Theological Seminary of Breslau. He obtained his PhD in 1871. In 1873 he was licensed to preach as a rabbi by Benjamin Artom in London. He served as preacher of the Great St Helen's Synagogue before moving to New York to preach to the Shaaray Tefillah congregation. In 1877 he was elected rabbi of the congregation and served in that position until 1920, when he retired as Rabbi Emeritus. Mendes acquired a great reputation for his scholarship and writings. In 1879 he founded the *American Hebrew* magazine, along with his brother Henry and others. In 1888 he wrote an article entitled "In Defense of Jehovah" for the *North American Review*. In 1900 he became revising editor of the *Jewish Encyclopaedia*, and in 1903 was appointed editor of the *Menorah*, a monthly magazine. Mendes was a biblical scholar, writing the *Child's First Bible*, and serving as one of the revisers for the Jewish Publication Society of America version of the Bible.

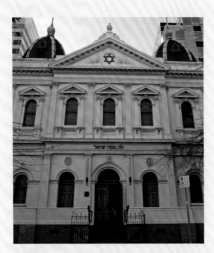

Solomon Mestel
Rabbi
1886–1966

Solomon Mestel was born in Brody, Galicia, now in Ukraine. He came to Britain in 1908, settling in London. He was educated at the University of London, matriculating in 1911. In 1914 he graduated BA honours in Hebrew and Aramaic. In 1919 he was awarded his MA. In the same year he married Rachel Brodetsky, sister of the mathematician Selig Brodetsky. Mestel began working as a minister of religion. In 1923 he emigrated to Australia, settling in Melbourne. He became minister of East Melbourne synagogue and was awarded semicha, a qualification whereby a Jewish man can become a rabbi, in 1926. At this time he also became an active Freemason. In the late 1920s Mestel joined the lobby led by the Judean League to keep the Sabbath sacred, in opposition to those who wanted to play sport on that day. In 1930 Mestel returned to London and was appointed rabbi at Forest Gate. He held this position until 1951. On retirement he devoted his time to scholarship, translating several legal tracts from Hebrew to English. Mestel's son was the renowned British astronomer Leon Mestel.

George Mikes

Known for his humorous
cultural commentaries
1912–1987

George Mikes was born in
Siklos, Hungary to Alfred
Mikes, a successful lawyer,
and Margo Halmos. Mikes
studied law and received a
doctorate from Budapest
University in 1933, after which he started working as a journalist
for *Reggel* newspaper. In 1938 he was sent to England as the
newspaper's London correspondent to cover the Munich Crisis; he
ended up staying his entire life. Mikes wrote for both English and
Hungarian publications, such as the *Observer*, the *Times Literary
Supplement, Irodalmi Újság* and *Népszava*. From 1939, he worked
as a documentary maker for the BBC Hungarian section, and, from
1975 until his death, he also worked for the Hungarian section of
Szabad Europa Radio. His first book, *We Were There To Escape* – the
true story of a Jugoslav officer – was published in 1945. His second
book, *How to be an Alien* (1946), which poked fun at the English,
went into 30 editions and established his reputation as a humourist
writer. His other notable cultural commentaries include *How to
Scrape Skies* (1948), *Milk and Honey: Israel Explored* (1950), *Italy
for Beginners* (1956) and *Switzerland for Beginners* (1962). He also
contributed to the BBC's satirical television comedy programme *That
Was The Week That Was*. His autobiography, *How To Be Seventy*, was
published on his 70th birthday.

Arnaldo Momigliano

Opened up a new area of
study for a new generation
1908–1987

Arnaldo Momigliano was born in
Cuneo, Italy to grain merchant
Riccardo and wife Ilda. The
family was prominent in Jewish
intellectual life in the early
20th century. Momigliano was
considered an expert in ancient history and authored his first work
on the Hellenistic Jewish book of the Maccabees in 1930. This was
followed by biographies of Claudius and Philip of Macedon. Due
to fascist persecution, Momigliano was fired from Turin University
and he travelled to Oxford in March 1939. He later taught at Bristol
University and University College London, where in 1951 he was
appointed Chair of Ancient History. Here, he established a new joint
degree in anthropology and ancient history. Momigliano is credited
with the creation of the new academic discipline of historiography. He
opened up this area of study to a new generation and his seminars
were attended by hundreds at a time. His wisdom on this new subject
is best shown in the posthumous work *The Classical Foundations of
Modern Historiography*. Momigliano lost his parents and other family
members in the Holocaust but retained his Jewish faith. He is buried
in the Jewish cemetery in Cuneo.

Ewen Montagu
Judge, naval intelligence
officer and writer
1901–1985

Ewen Edward Samuel Montagu
was born in Kensington, London.
He was the son of Louis Samuel
Montagu, second Baron
Swaythling, and Gladys Helen
Rachel. He was educated at
Westminster School, and graduated from Trinity College, Cambridge
in 1923. Montagu was called to the bar from the Middle Temple in
1924 and became a King's Counsel in 1939. A keen yachtsman, he
accepted a commission in the Royal Naval reserves, and in 1941 was
transferred to the intelligence division. There his best-known mission
was Operation Mincemeat, a dazzlingly audacious plan to place
misleading intelligence in the hands of the enemy. Documents were
placed on what appeared to be the body of a Royal Marines officer,
which indicated an imminent attack on Sardinia rather than Sicily. When
the ruse worked, the famous message came back to high command
that "Mincemeat had been swallowed whole". After the war Montagu
enjoyed a new career as a non-fiction writer, entirely by accident. In
order to prevent the release of a potentially sensitive novel about
Operation Mincemeat, Montagu wrote his own account in response to
an appeal from the Admiralty. As *The Man Who Never Was* (1953) the
book sold over 2 million copies and inspired a film of the same name
in 1955. In 1977 Montagu wrote a more wide-ranging autobiography
of his wartime experiences entitled *Beyond Top Secret U* (1977). He was
appointed OBE in recognition of his work on Operation Mincemeat.

Claude Montefiore

Scholar and founder
of Liberal Judaism
1858–1938

Claude Joseph Goldsmid
Montefiore was born in London.
His parents were Nathaniel
Mayer Montefiore, a medical
practitioner, and Emma née
Goldsmid. Montefiore was the
sprig of two very wealthy family trees. He was educated privately and
then went up to Balliol College, Oxford. In 1881 he graduated with a
first in Classics. Montefiore began to reject the tenets of Orthodox
Judaism, and embrace the concept of denationalised and deritualised
Judaism. He preached the founding principles of Liberal Judaism from
the pulpit of the West London Synagogue on 1 February 1896. He
was persuaded by reformer Lily Montagu of the virtue of forming
an organisation to promote his views, and on 16 February 1902
the Jewish Religious Union was born. Montefiore was an implacable
anti-Zionist. He signed a letter to *The Times* in 1917 that stated
that the Jews were not a homeless people and that they had no
national aspirations. It wasn't the last controversial pronouncement
Montefiore would make. He later blamed Zionism for Hitler's rise to
power. Montefiore wrote widely on religious subjects and served as
the joint editor of the *Jewish Quarterly Review*. His major work was
his *Bible for Home Reading* (1897), which went into three editions.
In the 1920s Montefiore was awarded honorary degrees from the
Universities of Manchester and Oxford, and in 1930 was awarded the
British Academy Medal for biblical studies.

Hugh Montefiore

A vicar not afraid to
speak his mind
1920–2005

Hugh Montefiore was born in
London to stockbroker Charles
Sebag-Montefiore and wife
Muriel Alice. His parents were
Sephardi Jews who attended
Lauderdale Synagogue in Maida
Vale. Montefiore was to be a rabbi until at the age of 16 he saw a
vision of a figure in white who commanded Montefiore to follow him.
Believing this figure to be Jesus, Montefiore converted to Christianity
and in 1949 he was ordained into the Church of England. Montefiore
became an expert in New Testament studies at Cambridge and
was later appointed Bishop of Birmingham. Montefiore was not
afraid to court controversy: in 1967 he delivered a lecture in
which he stated that it was unusual that Jesus remained unmarried
and then suggested that perhaps Jesus had been homosexual.
He later described the lecture as having caused a "colossal
scandal." Montefiore campaigned on a wide range of issues including
climate change and nuclear disarmament. He attempted to introduce
his own "Infant Life Preservation Bill" into the House of Lords, which
called for the abortion limit to be reduced from 28 to 24 weeks. He
continually re-examined his own beliefs and described himself as an
exile from the Jewish community who was not quite accepted in the
Christian world.

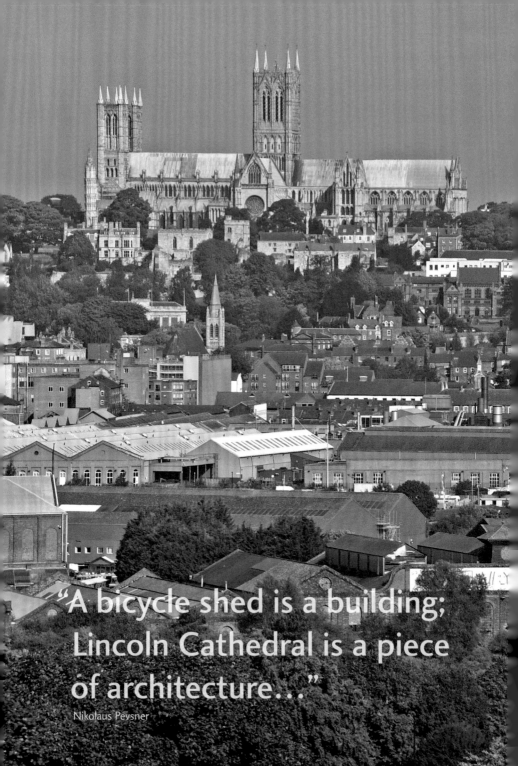

"A bicycle shed is a building;
Lincoln Cathedral is a piece
of architecture…"

Nikolaus Pevsner

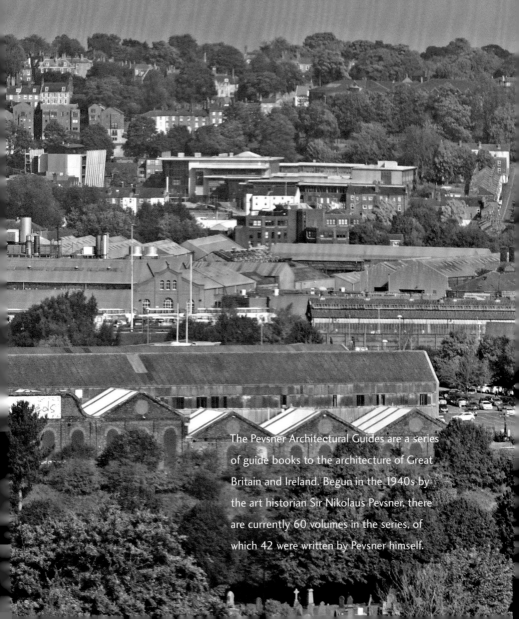

The Englishness of
a Jewish Émigré…

The Pevsner Architectural Guides are a series
of guide books to the architecture of Great
Britain and Ireland. Begun in the 1940s by
the art historian Sir Nikolaus Pevsner, there
are currently 60 volumes in the series, of
which 42 were written by Pevsner himself.

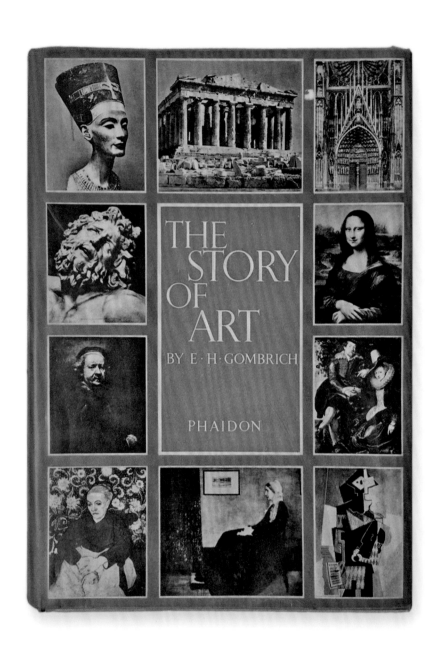

Ernst Gombrich, *The Story of Art*, Phaidon, 1950.

The Englishness of a Jewish Émigré: Nikolaus Pevsner and the History of Architecture

Joe Kerr
Architectural historian

When I was offered a place to read the history of art nearly four decades ago, the two books that were required reading before commencing my studies were *The Story of Art* by Ernst Gombrich and *An Outline of European Architecture* by Nikolaus Pevsner. What is remarkable about the selection of these two texts as essential primers for an English art history degree is that both were written by Jewish exiles, from Austria and Germany respectively. While both texts were admittedly rather outdated by the time I was required to read them, their enduring reputations speak volumes about the extraordinary influence that their German-speaking authors had exerted on British scholarship since their arrival here in the 1930s. Indeed, the study of art history, which at that time was barely established as an academic discipline in this country, was ultimately transformed into a respectable and respected enterprise by the intellectual rigour and methodological expertise of a distinguished group of Jewish *Mittel-European* scholars that also included Rudolf Wittkower, Edgar Wind and Aby Warburg (whose posthumous legacy was bestowed on London when his research institute was relocated there from Hamburg in 1933).

The Story of Art (1950) was destined to become the bestselling art historical book of all time, and upon his death in 2001 Gombrich was described by the *New York Times* as "probably the world's best-known art historian". While Pevsner may not ever have achieved a comparable international appeal, what makes his career so intriguing is that he not only established himself as a leading architectural historian with such survey texts as *The Outline of European Architecture,* but that he also became the most celebrated authority on the history of British, and especially English, architecture in the years after the Second World War. In particular, his magisterial *Buildings of England* series of county-by-county architectural guides, of which he wrote 32 volumes himself and a further 10 with collaborators between 1951 and 1974, cemented his enduring reputation as the essential companion to any architectural excursion in this country; the individual volumes are invariably referred to by their users simply as "Pevsners" in testament to the genius of their author. This impressive achievement is rendered all the more extraordinary by the fact that Pevsner was on the face of it a singularly inauspicious candidate to become the leading authority on any aspect of British culture; and it is the reasons why this is so that provide ample justification for focusing on his academic career in the context of this book.

To comprehend Pevsner's singular ineligibility for his eventual role as the interpreter of English architecture for the English themselves, one has to understand something of his intellectual formation in Germany in the years immediately after the First World War. As his biographer Susan Harries recounts, Pevsner was as a young man profoundly ill at ease with "the atmosphere and values of the Weimar Republic" (*Nikolaus Pevsner: The Life,* 2013). Equally, he "did not feel Jewish, nor did he wish to be a Jew". Instead, Pevsner was baptised into the Lutheran church in 1921 and he matured into an ardent German nationalist. He believed strongly in the authentic expression of a German identity through German art, opinions that brought his own world view into uncomfortably close proximity with Nazi pronouncements on art and art history. The Pevsner scholar Stephen Games has argued that Pevsner displayed a clear and definite sympathy with certain aspects of National Socialist ideology. He cites a conversation in 1933 in which Pevsner explained: "I love Germany, it is my country. I am a Nationalist, and in spite of the way I am treated, I want this movement to succeed… There are worse things than Hitlerism." Scholarly opinion is divided on just how serious or profound Pevsner's Nazi sympathies were, beyond a distaste for liberalism and a naïve optimism that Hitler's economic programme might lift Germany out of its financial and cultural predicament. Harries avoids an outright condemnation of his beliefs with the face-saving suggestion that "Pevsner's motives are certainly not clear to us now, and may not have been entirely clear to him then." However, the reality was that in 1933 Pevsner found himself excluded from a culture that he had so unequivocally identified himself with on the grounds of an identity and heritage that he had absolutely rejected, and thus was forced to take refuge in an alien country with which he felt very little empathy.

Pevsner's unfortunate sympathies for an ideology that had now repulsed him proved no impediment to building a successful career in the country that was eventually to prove itself wholly opposed to Nazi Germany. Once settled in England, and through the agency of influential friends, he developed a somewhat precarious portfolio of varied but overlapping careers as an academic, a journalist, a commercial buyer for a furniture showroom and a broadcaster and public commentator. As an art historian rigorously trained within a fully formed academic discipline, he rightly saw himself as far in advance of the amateur connoisseurship that passed for art historical scholarship in this country. It was armed with this perception of himself as a professional historian in a land of ill-informed dilettantes that he began his long and prolific career as the writer of authoritative but genuinely popular histories of architecture and design that were to shape the British understanding of these subjects in the decades after the Second World War, and which continue to exert an influence today.

Arno Breker, *The Torch Bearer*, 1939. The Nazi view that art should embody an inner racial ideal was supported by Pevsner to the point he was called "more German than the Germans".

Walter Gropius, Bauhaus building, 1926. Pevsner eschewed British architecture of the early 20th century in favour of European modernist movements such as the Bauhaus.

Pioneers of the Modern Movement – From William Morris to Walter Gropius, published in 1936, posited a direct connection between the two cultures that he now straddled, by charting the transmission of ideas from one to the other – albeit in reverse order to his own movement between the two. It also articulated for the first time in English his Hegelian-infused theory of historical progress and change, determined by the notion of the *zeitgeist* or spirit of the age. Under this historiographic model the *zeitgeist* was understood as the overwhelming and inescapable force that controlled and determined all cultural output. It posited the task of the historian as exposing the impact of the *zeitgeist* on the art and architecture of each age. As he was to write later in *Outline*: "Architecture is not the product of materials and purposes – nor by the way of social conditions – but of the changing spirits of changing ages." Furthermore, it proposed that in any given epoch the *zeitgeist* reaches its most perfect and novel expression in only one place and culture, and passes like a relay baton through history, impelled forward by a relentless dialectic cycle of action followed by reaction. Thus it progresses forward towards whatever the historian identifies as the authentic expression of his own age – which in Pevsner's case meant the German Modernism of the Bauhaus.

This deterministic and cyclical model of cultural history provided the necessary framework for Pevsner to write his great survey, *An Outline of European Architecture*, which embraced over 1,500 years of architectural history in little more than a couple of hundred paperback pages. This concentration was only made possible because it allowed him to trace the course of the *zeitgeist* as it passed from one country to another, and only certain countries at that:

> *Whoever makes up his mind to write a short history of European architecture, or art, or philosophy, or drama, or agriculture, must*

*decide in which part of Europe at any time those things happened
which seem to him to express most intensely the vital will and vital
feelings of Europe. It is for this reason that, e.g. Germany is not
mentioned for her 16th-century but for her 18th-century buildings,
that Spain's role in Western Mohammedan architecture is left
out, but her role in Western Christian architecture considered,
that buildings in the Netherlands are only touched upon, and
Scandinavian buildings not mentioned at all.*

As with his earlier *Pioneers of the Modern Movement,* the culmination of
this book is provided by the decisive shift of the *zeitgeist* from the Britain
of John Ruskin, William Morris and the Arts and Crafts movement to the
Germany of Walter Gropius and the Bauhaus. This moment is marked
by one of the most extraordinary and arresting assertions ever to be
made about British architecture, namely that: "For the next 40 years,
the first 40 of our century, no British name need here be mentioned.
Britain had led Europe and America in architecture and design for a
long time; now her ascendancy had come to an end." And so this recent
émigré dismissed the contemporary architecture of the country that had
offered him asylum, in favour of the architecture of the country that had
rejected him – and which had now also rejected the very Modernism
that he espoused. Furthermore, at the time he wrote these words in
1942, those countries were locked in combat to determine the future
of the very continent whose architectural past Pevsner was mapping.

Given this continued adherence to a philosophy of history that
enabled him to reject wholesale the greater part of the architectural
history of England, what followed next in Pevsner's professional
development is all the more remarkable. For in 1945 he was
commissioned to undertake the greatest single endeavour of his or any
other architectural historian's career, namely to research and write *The*

Buildings of England series for Penguin Books. Clearly, this project could not be framed by the same philosophy of history that had underpinned his previous academic *oeuvre*, as it required a methodical and empirical examination of the entirety of English architecture, and not merely those few periods that conformed to the spirit of the age. Regardless, Pevsner applied his rigorous and methodical research skills to a process that was to occupy him off and on for nearly three decades, by which time he had surveyed and described upwards of 30,000 individual buildings. What is delightful to find in reading his often brief but usually measured entries is the growing fascination and engagement with English architecture that characterised his later career, writing as he did with genuine warmth and affection for the quirky details of medieval parish churches, or of the grand sweep of picturesque landscape compositions. At times, his judgements can be wickedly brutal or nakedly polemical, as with his comment in the Middlesex volume, the very first to be published:

Wood Green: The Inventory of the Royal Commission says, "No monuments known", and there is indeed nothing in the borough worth more than a cursory glance.

At other times, his objective judgement is noticeably clouded by the reassertion of his Hegelian historiography, to the point that he ties himself in intellectual knots. This is exemplified in his entry for St Catherine's College, Oxford, by the Modernist master Arne Jacobson, a building that Pevsner seems driven to justify. His opening sentence reads, "Here is a perfect piece of architecture", a proposition possibly not shared by all of its sun-baked residents – and even to defend against the suspicion that a building designed by a Dane might be "un-English".

The *Buildings of England* series is an outstanding achievement by any standards. It certainly suffices to cement Pevsner's place in the pantheon of distinguished Jewish émigrés who have so enriched the intellectual culture of this country since their arrival over 80 years ago. Perhaps the role it has played in illuminating the richness of English architecture to an English audience goes some way to ameliorating Pevsner's disconcerting flirtation with ideas being promulgated within Nazi Germany. But it must not ever be allowed to suppress or conceal the evidence for Pevsner's ultra-nationalist beliefs. Indeed, it is important to understand that Pevsner adhered to some of those beliefs throughout his long career, and not merely his unshakeable belief in the Bauhaus functionalism of his native interwar Germany. For instance, his famous series of Reith Lectures delivered for the BBC in 1955, and entitled *The Englishness of English Art* (to which the title of this essay refers) reasserts his belief in a geography of art based on "underlying assumptions about permanent national 'spirits' and racial types". These are ideas so close to Nazi ideology as to have been unthinkable in Germany at this time, but whose oblique political overtones his English audience failed to notice.

Pevsner remains an enigmatic figure within this larger story of Jewish thinkers in this country. He made an undeniable and enduring contribution to intellectual life generally, and to the proper establishment of the academic discipline of art history, based on his rigorous German training. He became an acknowledged expert in the history of English architecture and was responsible for one of the greatest achievements in this field. But as Susan Harries observes, "he was not English … and never wanted to be." It may be a long time before we can reach a definitive verdict on Pevsner the thinker, and Pevsner the man.

Arne Jacobsen, St Catherine's College, Oxford, 1962, described by Pevsner in the *Buildings of England* book series as "a perfect piece of architecture".

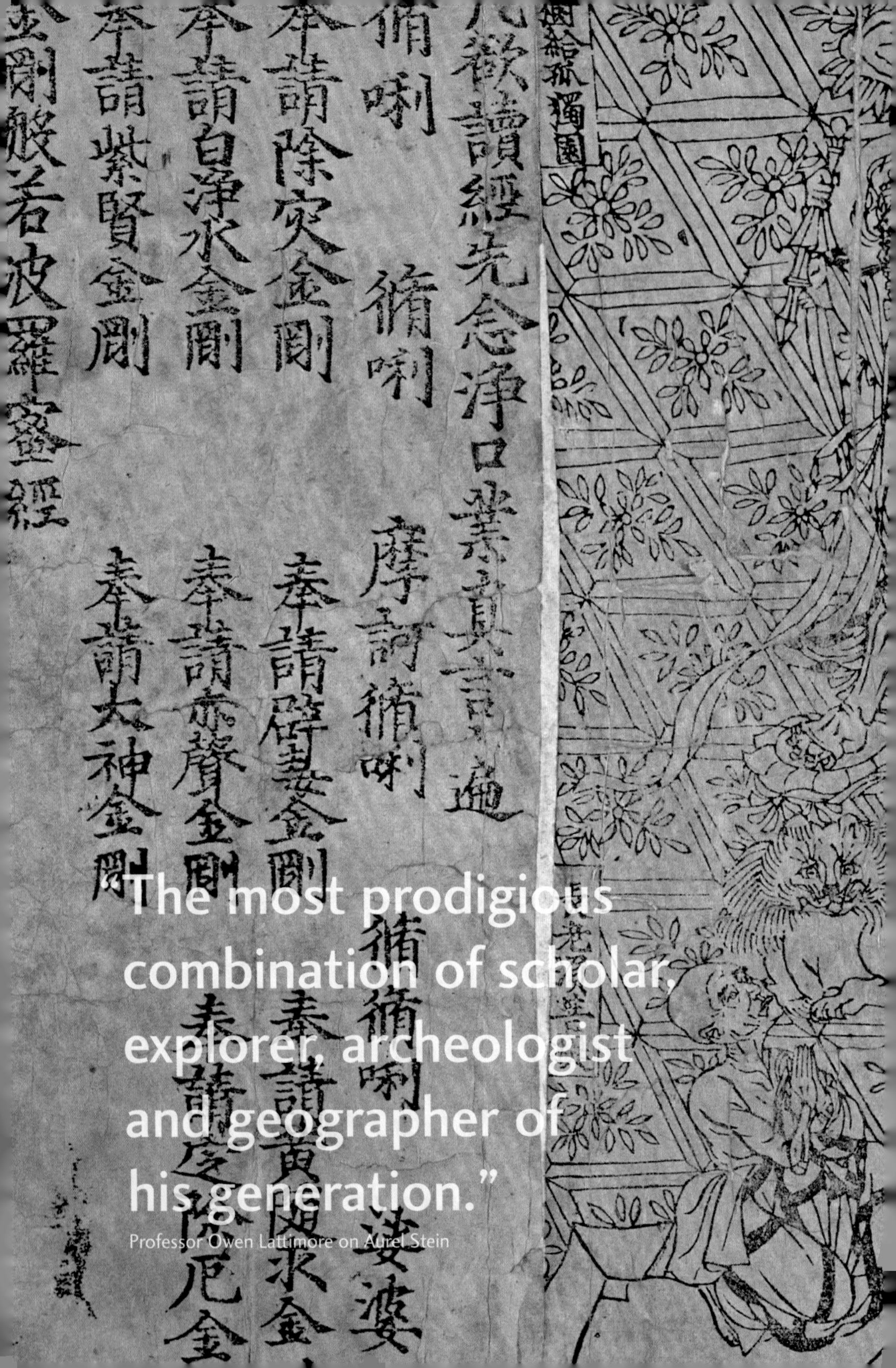

國稱孤樓圖

八歡讀經先念淨口業真言通

循唎

循唎

摩訶循唎

奉請辟妄金剛

奉請亦聲金剛

循循唎

奉請黃□水金

婆婆

奉請除災金剛

奉請白淨水金剛

李請紫賢金剛

李請大神金剛

金剛般若波羅蜜經

The most prodigious combination of scholar, explorer, archeologist and geographer of his generation."

Professor Owen Lattimore on Aurel Stein

Biographies N – Z

The *Diamond Sutra* is a Bhuddist teaching that has been translated into a variety of languages over a broad geographic range. A copy of a Tang-dynasty Chinese version was found in the Cave of the Thousand Buddhas in 1907 by Aurel Stein. Inscribed 11 May 868 it is, said to be the earliest complete survival of a dated printed book.

Lewis Bernstein Namier
Historian
1888–1960

Lewis Bernstein Namier was born Ludwik Neimirowski in Russian Poland to Joseph Neimirowski and his wife Anne. The family were assimilated into Polish life but Namier retained a lifelong dislike of Jews who, desiring assimilation, hid their Jewish identity. He was driven away from Lvov University by antisemitism and forged a career in England. During the First World War he served with the British Army and later the Propaganda Department, the Department of Information and the Foreign Office. He remained at the latter until 1920, and played an important role in post-war discussions regarding the territories of the newly created independent Polish state. A lifelong Zionist, Namier worked as political secretary for the Jewish Agency in Palestine (1929–31), and was a friend and associate of Chaim Weizmann.

He is best known today as an expert on 18th-century politics. His pioneering *The Structure of Politics at the Ascension of George III* (1929) made use of hitherto unused sources. It also earned him the position of chair of modern history at Manchester University. Other notable academic publications included *England in the Age of the American Revolution* (1930) and the *History of Parliament* series (1940). He was an active figure in the anti-appeasement movement during the 1930s, together with his protégé the historian A. J. P. Taylor. In 1947 Namier converted to Anglicanism to marry his second wife. He was knighted in 1952.

Adolf Neubauer
Discoverer of lost manuscripts
1831 – 1907

Adolf Neubauer was born in Hungary to Jacob and Amalie. His father was a merchant and Talmudic scholar who wanted his son to become a rabbi. However, in 1857 while living in Paris, Adolf became fascinated by the discovery and analysis of medieval Hebrew manuscripts. After the publication of his *La Geographie du Talmud*, a study of the geographical locations found within the Talmud, Neubauer moved to Oxford. He worked in the Bodleian Library cataloguing Hebrew manuscripts and became responsible for dramatically enlarging the library's collection of original religious texts. In the late 1890s Neubauer realised the importance of collections of Hebrew material attached to synagogues, known as genizahs. He obtained nearly 3,000 manuscripts from the genizot of the Ben Ezra Synagogue in Cairo and brought them to Oxford. Neubauer was also the first to discover a fragment from the original Hebrew book of Ecclesiasticus. A prolific writer, Neubauer is well remembered for his two-volume history on the writings of French rabbis, which utilised sources from unpublished manuscripts all over Europe. Neubauer was regarded as an Englishman and was completely integrated into Oxford life. He was religiously unobservant but dedicated his life to uncovering the value of lost Jewish literature.

David Nieto

Rabbi and scholar

1654–1728

David Nieto was born in Venice. He was the son of Phineas Nieto. David studied medicine in Padua and then worked as a dayan (religious judge), preacher and physician in Leghorn. His first work *Pascalogia* (1693) demonstrated his intellectual interest in astronomy and calendration. In 1701 Nieto was called to London to serve as the haham of the Sephardi congregation at the newly built Bevis Marks synagogue. In that capacity he founded an orphanage in 1703 and a society for visiting the sick in 1709. In 1703 one of Nieto's sermons saw him entangled in a theological controversy involving the separation of nature and God. He was accused of heresy and forced to explain his viewpoint in *De la divina providencia* (1704) He was cleared of all charges in 1705. He continued to write on Jewish doctrine and law, publishing his most noted work *Matteh Dan veKuzari helek sheni* (*Rod of Dan and the second Kuzari*) in 1714. Nieto moved in intellectual circles that included the physician and philosopher Jacob de Castro Sarmento and the poet Daniel Lopez Laguna, and though he never learned English to the degree that he could write scholarly texts in that language, he became well versed in Greek and Roman classics. His son Isaac Nieto succeeded him as haham of Bevis Marks.

Isaac Nieto
Rabbi and scholar
1702–1744

Isaac Nieto was born in London. He was the son of David Nieto, haham of the Bevis Marks Synagogue. In 1733, following his father's death, Isaac was officially appointed his successor as hakham ha-shalem of Bevis Marks. He gave up the post in 1741 when he travelled abroad. On his return in 1747 he found work as a notary. In 1749 Nieto travelled to Gibraltar and established the Shaar Hashamayim congregation. Thus he became Gibraltar's first rabbi and founded the oldest synagogue on the island, known as the Great Synagogue. In 1751 he was called back to his London congregation to accept the appointment of ab bet din. In 1756 he preached a *Sermon Moral* that was subsequently published in Spanish and English. He translated the prayer book in two volumes, and his work became the basis of all further translations. Nieto became embroiled in a dispute with the fellow members of his bet din and resigned in 1757.

Alexander Nove
Leading expert in Soviet studies
1915–1994

Alexander Nove was born in St Petersburg, Russia. His parents were both Jewish. The whole family left Russia in the wake of the 1917 revolution. They changed the family name from Novakovsky and moved to England. Alexander attended King Alfred School in London and then studied for a BSc in economics at the London School of Economics. After graduating, Nove served in the army and climbed the ranks to Major in intelligence. He worked on the Board of Trade from 1947 as a specialist in Soviet affairs, and was permitted to spend two years at the University of Glasgow's Soviet Studies department. In 1958 Nove became reader in Russian social and economic studies at the LSE and in 1963 took the James Bonar Chair of Economics at the University of Glasgow in addition to becoming the director of its Institute of Soviet and East European Studies. Nove's experiences in the army and the British civil service gave him a unique insight into the functioning of the Soviet system, and he demonstrated the internal struggles behind the unified facade in his highly regarded work. Nove was not religious and put his happiness and success down to luck rather than divine intervention.

Francis Palgrave

Historian and archivist
who helped create the
Public Record Office
1788–1861

Born Francis Ephraim Cohen in
London, Palgrave was the son
of Meyer (a stockbroker) and
Rachel. Interested in history
from a young age, he combined
his work as a solicitor's clerk between 1803 and 1822 with regular
contributions on historical and literary themes to the *Edinburgh
Review* and the *Quarterly Review*. He converted to Christianity shortly
before his marriage to Elizabeth Turner in 1823, changing his name
to Palgrave, the maiden name of his mother-in-law. In 1827 Palgrave
was admitted to the bar, but was increasingly engaged in editing and
publishing transcriptions of historical records and archives. In 1834
he became keeper of records at the Chapter House in Westminster,
at the time a repository for nationally important records such as
the Domesday Book. The near destruction of the Chapter House
by fire in 1834 contributed to calls for the establishment of a Public
Record Office, eventually created by an Act of Parliament in 1838.
Palgrave was appointed as its deputy keeper and would remain until
his death in1861, overseeing the transfer, ordering and cataloguing
of vast numbers of records, many in poor condition, to prepare them
for public access. Palgrave also authored several historical works,
including 1832's *The Rise and Progress of the English Commonwealth*,
and was knighted in the same year.

Joseph Pardo

Author of *Shulhan Tahor*

1624–1677

Joseph Pardo was born in Amsterdam, Netherlands. His father, David ben Joseph Pardo, was a Dutch rabbi and haham, a Hebrew scholar. He moved to London, where he served as Reader at the Spanish and Portuguese congregation. Joseph succeeded his father at the congregation. It was there that he wrote *Shulhan Tahor*, a compendium of the first two parts of Joseph Caro's *Shulhan 'Aruk*. This was edited by his son, David, and published in Amsterdam in 1686. It was dedicated to the "Kaal Kados De Londres" (Holy Community of London). Pardo was married and had two children, his son David and daughter Rachel. He died in Amsterdam and was buried in the same grave as his grandfather, an Italian rabbi of the same name, at Beth Haim in Ouderkerk aan de Amstel, Netherlands.

Nikolaus Pevsner

German art historian
who revealed British
architecture to the British
1902–1983

Born in Leipzig, Pevsner was the
youngest son of Russian migrants
Hugo Pewsner (a fur trader) and
Annie Perlmann. He showed early
academic promise, and studied at
the Universities of Leipzig, Munich, Berlin and Frankfurt (completing
his thesis on the Baroque merchant houses of his home city). In 1928
he took up a post at the University of Göttingen, but was forced out
because of his Jewish background when the Nazis came to power in
1933, despite the fact he had converted to Lutheranism in 1921 and
had initially supported many aspects of National Socialism. That year
he left for Britain (his wife and three children did not join him until
1935), taking up a post at the University of Birmingham. In 1940 he
was briefly interned as an enemy alien in Huyton but in 1942 was
appointed Lecturer at Birkbeck College, remaining there until 1969.
Holding interests as he did in a range of subject matters, Pevsner's
work could broadly be described as exploring the impact of national
character on art and architecture. In 1945 he began work on a series
of county-by-county architectural guides to Britain that would make
him a household name. The first three volumes were launched in
1951, and the 46 volumes were completed (with the help of several
collaborators) by 1974. Initially known as *The Buildings of England*,
the guides were renamed *Pevsner Architectural Guides* in 1998. He was
knighted for services to art and architecture in 1969.

Alexander Piatigorsky

One of Russia's greatest
philosophers
1929–2009

Alexander Piatigorsky was a
philosopher and expert in south
Asian culture. Born in the Soviet
Union, he did not show early
academic promise, being expelled
from school twice. Regardless
of this he managed to master eight languages, including Sanskrit
and Tamil, as well as immersing himself in Asian philosophy and
thought. During the 1960s he became involved with the Moscow
School of Methodology, which is now considered to have been one
of the most influential schools of philosophical thought. At the time,
however, it operated in secret behind the Iron Curtain. His *Symbol
and Consciousness: Metaphysical Discussion of Consciousness, Symbolism
and Language* examined the idea of consciousness, drawing on theory
from both western and eastern schools of thought. The work was
smuggled out of the Soviet Union by Ernest Gellner and is regarded
as one of the most important philosophical texts of the last century.
Piatigorsky held a professorship at the School of Oriental and African
Studies at the University of London and wrote three philosophical
novels. As a Jew studying Buddhism, Piatigorsky drew suspicion from
the Soviet authorities, so he would conduct debates with colleagues
in Sanskrit. He valued his Jewish upbringing and would say "I am a
Jew; a very bad Jew."

N – Z

Michael Polanyi
Found a place for
religion in science
1891 – 1976

Michael Polanyi was a chemist
and political philosopher. He was
born to Mihaly Polacsek and his
wife Cecilia in Budapest. In 1919
Polanyi fled to Germany as a
result of antisemitism spread by
revolutionary forces during the collapse of the communist regime
in Hungary. In Germany, Polanyi specialised in physical chemistry.
His work on thermodynamics brought him into contact with Albert
Einstein. The rise of Nazism forced Polanyi to move again, this time to
the University of Manchester. Here Polanyi began to concentrate on
political philosophy and in 1940 he published his first philosophical
work, *The Contempt of Freedom*, which led to his appointment as chair
of social studies at Manchester. Polanyi's best-known work, *Personal
Knowledge*, argued against the established scientific approach of
investigation through rational, objective enquiry. Instead, he argued
that investigations should begin with the researcher's hunches
or feelings (what he termed tacit knowledge) and all objective
examination should follow on from this. Although Polanyi described
himself as a "non-Jewish Jew" and was baptised into Catholicism, his
Jewish heritage and commitment to a belief in God influenced his
desire to fuse the religious and the scientific worlds.

Karl Popper

He declared scientific theory
to be best when proven false
1902–1994

Karl Popper was born into
the Viennese intelligentsia,
to parents Simon and Jenny.
Popper's maternal grandparents
ran an orphanage in Vienna
during the 1900s and one
infamous resident was a young Adolf Hitler. In his early years Popper
flitted from musical studies to manual labour before settling on the
field of philosophy. He moved to Britain in 1946, taking up a post at
the London School of Economics, before moving to the University
of London in 1949. After listening to Einstein explain his theory of
relativity, Popper realised that the most important part of scientific
discovery was the capacity for scientists to realise that theories could
be proven false. He believed that scientists must continually test their
ideas; and, if refuted, they must adapt their hypotheses or establish
a new theory altogether. Popper maintained that any investigations
that did not follow this logic were non-scientific. Popper had a
rather difficult personality, which often resulted in heated exchanges
with colleagues. One story has become legend: during a debate
with Ludwig Wittgenstein, Popper angered the other philosopher
so much that Wittgenstein raised a hot poker to Popper before
storming off. Regardless of his at-times problematic personality traits,
Popper was much admired and Margaret Thatcher regarded him as
her intellectual mentor. In 1985 Popper briefly returned to Austria,
but he retired to Surrey in 1986.

Michael Postan

He augmented our understanding
of British economic history
1899–1981

Economic historian Michael
Postan was born in Bessarabia
(modern-day Moldova) to
Efim Postan and his wife Elena.
Although Postan attempted
to study at various Russian
universities, army service and the Russian Revolution continually
disrupted his education and he left Russia in 1919. Arriving in Britain
in 1920, he enrolled at the London School of Economics. Postan
is remembered as one of the most influential economic historians
of the 20th century. In addition to holding academic positions at
the LSE, University College London and Cambridge, he is credited
with devising the "Postan thesis" about economics during the
Middle Ages. Postan argued that in rural 14th-century England, the
increasing population faced economic and resource insufficiencies
that were greatly eased by the Great Plague. His arguments were
outlined in the 1952 *Cambridge Economic History of Europe*. Postan
wrote a number of other economic histories of western Europe and
contributed to Britain's official civil history of the Second World War.
He was a popular teacher and Eric Hobsbawm remembered him as
"one of the greatest lecturers at Cambridge." The nature of Postan's
relationship with Judaism is not exactly known, but his ability to
adapt to his new surroundings by forging a new identity may have
contributed to his success.

Sigbert Prais

Analysed the post-war decline
in British productivity
1928–2014

Sigbert Prais was born in
Frankfurt-am-Main, Germany.
His parents were Orthodox Jews
and the family fled to Britain in
1934 to escape the Nazis. Prais
was educated at King Edward's
School in Birmingham. He then took a degree in commerce at the
University of Birmingham before doing his PhD in applied economics
at Fitzwilliam College, Cambridge. He collaborated with American
economist Hendrik Houtthaker on the "Analysis of Family Budgets",
a highly influential paper that earned Prais a lecturing position at
Fitzwilliam. Prais took up a fellowship in Chicago with the influential
Cowles Commission for Research in Economics in 1953. There he
met C. B. Winsten, with whom he developed the Prais–Winsten
estimation, their equation for estimating the linear model. Prais
returned to London in 1954 and commenced a long-held position
with the National Institute of Economic and Social Research. He left
academia in the 1960s to work as the finance director of his father's
manufacturing business. His later academic work tried to explain the
decline in British productivity by comparison with other countries
in Europe. Prais argued that training played a crucial role. Prais gave
each of his children a traditional German *schultüte* (a cone filled with
sweets) on their first day of school to make up for missing out on
the rite himself.

Marjorie Proops

Britain's popular agony aunt
1911 – 1996

Marjorie Proops was born
Rebecca Marjorie Israel in
London to father Abraham
Israel and his wife Martha
Flatau. Her father changed
his name to Alfred Rayle in
order to avoid antisemitism
within the business world and Marjorie remembered encountering
antisemitic insults at school. During the war years she penned a
weekly column for *Good Taste* magazine about the wartime struggles
of motherhood. She is best known for her advice column, which she
began writing for the *Daily Herald* in 1950. As her popularity grew,
Proops, or Marje as she was known to her readers, moved to the
Women's Mirror and finally to the *Daily Mirror.* Her advice reflected
the changing norms in society. Beginning in the 1950s, she
explained how a woman might best please her husband, and ended
her career by encouraging women to expect more from love and
careers. She was a vocal campaigner for minority rights and in 1994
took part in a petition to lower the homosexual age of consent to
16. Proops described herself as British first and Jewish second. She
married her husband Sidney in a synagogue and received a Jewish
burial at Golders Green Jewish Cemetery.

Claire Rayner

Voice of the sexual revolution
1931–2010

Claire Rayner was born in the East End of London to parents Percy and Betty. She always knew she wanted to work in healthcare and at 14 attempted to be a nurse at Epsom Cottage Hospital before her real age was discovered. She was best known for her health advice and agony aunt columns in various British publications. Beginning in 1962 for *Hers* magazine and also writing for both the *Sun* and the *Daily Mirror*, Rayner dealt with a vast range of the nation's problems. She wrote in an extremely accessible style and was not afraid to lift the lid on sexual taboos. She once famously demonstrated how to use a condom on live TV – the first person ever to do so. As a nurse, she campaigned for better conditions for health practitioners as well as for medical law reform. Rayner argued for free contraception, better sex education and freedom of choice in regard to abortion. By the end of her life she was a patron of over 100 charities. Rayner was an outspoken atheist who requested a humanist burial service.

John Rodker

Publisher and translator
1894–1955

Rodker was born in Manchester, the son of a Polish immigrant and corset-maker. While Rodker was still a child, the family moved to the East End of London. He left school at 14 and became associated with the "Whitechapel Boys", a group of young Jewish writers and artists who met at the Whitechapel Art Gallery. By this point Rodker had decided to pursue a literary career, with his poetry and essays appearing in a number of publications. During the First World War Rodker's claim to be a conscientious objector was rejected, and he was imprisoned at Dartmoor. Following the war he devoted most of his working life to publishing and translation. In 1919, Rodker established the Ovid Press (with his first wife, novelist Mary Butts), a short-lived but influential printing press that published modernist writers and artists such as T. S. Eliot, Ezra Pound and Wyndham Lewis. This was followed in the 1920s by the Casanova Society, which published limited editions. Following a period of bankruptcy, he set up another short-lived company, the Pushkin Press, in 1937. Reflecting his strong interest in psychoanalysis, he established the Imago Publishing Company in 1938, collaborating with Anna Freud to publish the collected works of Sigmund Freud. Fluent in French, Rodker produced French translations of the work of James Joyce and also translated French writers such as Jean-Paul Sartre into English. He was posthumously awarded the *Légion d'honneur* by the French government.

Harold Rosen
Educationalist
1919–2008

Harold Rosen was born in Massachusetts and was raised by his mother in London's East End following her separation from Harold's father when he was just two years old. He followed in the family tradition of two generations of socialist activism, joining the Young Communist League in 1935 and participating in the Battle of Cable Street the following year. In 1940 Rosen graduated from University College London with a degree in English, and went into teaching. Still a US citizen, he was drafted into the US Army in 1945 and served in the Education Corps for two years, stationed in Frankfurt and Berlin. Following the war he resumed his teaching career, and in 1956 was made Head of English at the newly established Walworth Comprehensive School. It was also during this period that Rosen became disillusioned with the Communist Party, eventually leaving in 1957 following the Soviet invasion of Hungary the previous year. After leaving Walworth in 1958 Rosen began to focus on teacher education, and it was in this field that he would have his greatest influence, combining a socialist ethos with a passion for teaching. Rosen wrote several books on education, the most influential of which are *Language, the Learner and the School* (1969, co-authored with Douglas Barnes) and *The Language of Primary School Children* (1973, co-authored with his wife Connie Rosen). His memoir, *Are You Still Circumcised?*, was published in 1999.

Cecil Roth

Established the Jewish
Museum in London
1899–1970

Cecil Roth was born in London
to Polish father Joseph and
mother Etty. He received a
traditional religious education
and was taught Hebrew by the
eminent scholar Jacob Mann. He
dedicated his life to highlighting and celebrating Jewish life. During
the Second World War, Roth penned a number of works including *The
History of the Jews in England*, The *History of Jews in Italy*, *The Jewish
Contribution to Civilisation* and *The Rise of Provincial Jewry*. These works
were designed to show the world the enormous value of the Jewish
people in the face of Nazi persecution. His work was noticed and it
was later revealed that Roth's name was listed in SS-General Walter
Schallenberg's "Black Book", a list of those designated for immediate
assassination if the Nazis were ever to invade Britain. From 1965 Roth
held the editorship of the *Encyclopaedia Judaica*. Upon retirement,
Roth settled in Israel. A special highlight of his career was his
establishment of the Jewish Museum in London in 1932 along with
Wilfred Samuel. In the year after his death 16 volumes of his work
were published and continue to be used by students today.

Raphael Samuel

Left wing historian who
encouraged collaborative
historical enquiry
1934–1996

Raphael Samuel was born in
1934 in London. His interest
in politics was nurtured by his
mother, a communist activist,
and his uncle Chimen Abramsky,
a historian of socialism. As a schoolboy he was a member of the
Communist Party's historians group, which included Eric Hobsbawm
and E. P. Thompson. In 1952 Samuel won a scholarship to Balliol
College, Oxford, where he was taught by Christopher Hill. In 1956,
he left the Communist Party following the Soviet invasion of Hungary
and co-founded the *Universities and Left Review*, a forerunner of
the *New Left Review*. In 1962 he began teaching at Ruskin College,
Oxford, where he was known for his popular "history workshops",
hugely influential in the development of "history from below". These
encouraged students to present their findings alongside established
academics, and eventually led to the establishment of the *History
Workshop Journal* in 1976. Samuel's published work ranged from
studies of quarry labourers to the criminal underworld of the East
End and the importance of memory in the study of history. A year
before his death, he became Professor of History at the University
of East London. The Raphael Samuel History Centre, which aims
to encourage the widest possible participation in historical study
and debate, was founded in his memory. He is buried in Highgate
Cemetery, not far from the grave of Karl Marx.

Isaac Schapera
Social anthropologist
1905–2003

Born in Garies, Cape Colony, Schapera first studied law at the University of Cape Town before switching to anthropology. He completed his doctorate at the London School of Economics, where he was greatly influenced by Bronisław Malinowski, a proponent of functionalism within the field of anthropology. In 1929 Schapera returned to South Africa to teach at the University of the Witwatersrand before taking up a position at the UCT. Much of Schapera's early work focused on the Khoisan people, but he became best known for his published studies of the Tswana people, making many trips to Bechuanaland (then a British protectorate, now Botswana). In 1950 Schapera was appointed to a chair at the LSE, where he would remain for the rest of his career. By this time world-renowned in his field, he served as Chair of the Association of Social Anthropologists from 1954 to 1957 and President of the Royal Anthropological Institute from 1961 to 1963, and was also made a fellow of the British Academy in 1958. Schapera also edited the journals and letters of David Livingstone, published in six volumes between 1959 and 1963. He remained active within academia after his retirement in 1969, and by the time of his death had lived to see many of his students become distinguished anthropologists.

Leonard Schapiro

Leading academic in the study of
the Soviet Union
1908–1983

Leonard Schapiro was born in
Glasgow but spent some of his
childhood in Latvia and Russia.
His father, Max, was from Riga
and his mother Leah was the
daughter of a Glaswegian rabbi.
In 1921 the family returned to Britain, settling in London. Schapiro
attended a number of East End synagogues, not for religious reasons
but because he appreciated their vibrant culture. After studying law
at University College London, he worked for the BBC's monitoring
service during the Second World War. This job, in addition to the
work he did in intelligence, instilled in him an interest in Soviet
literature and history. In 1955 he published *The Origin of Communist
Autocracy*, a review of Soviet abuses of power that earned him
an academic position at the London School of Economics. This
was followed by his *The Communist Party of the Soviet Union*, in
which Schapiro drew a link between Stalinist policy and earlier
Leninist thought. Although many disagreed with this viewpoint, the
subsequent opening of the Soviet archives supported Schapiro's
ideas. Schapiro was not a practising Jew but felt close to aspects of
many different religions. He was, however, Chairman of the Board
of Soviet Jewish Affairs, an organisation dedicated to exposing the
Soviet Union's antisemitism.

Solomon Marcus Schiller-Szinessy

Rabbi and scholar
1820–1890

Born in Altofen, Hungary, Schiller-Szinessy gained a doctorate in philosophy and mathematics from the University of Jena, subsequently becoming ordained as a rabbi. He was the first Jew to be appointed to the faculty of the Lutheran Evangelical College in Eperjes (now Prešov, Slovakia). During the 1848 Hungarian Revolution he supported the revolutionaries, carrying out an order to blow up the bridge at Szeged, thereby halting the advance of the Austrian army. He was taken prisoner but avoided execution by escaping, fleeing first to Trieste and then to Ireland. Arriving in mainland Britain, Schiller-Szinessy was appointed minister of the United Congregation of Manchester and following the congregational split in 1857 accepted the position of minister at the newly formed Manchester Reform Synagogue. Despite modernist inclinations, Schiller-Szinessy maintained an Orthodox outlook and resigned from the position in 1860. In 1863 he moved to Cambridge to teach and to study the Hebrew manuscripts at the library there, later publishing *Catalogue of the Hebrew Manuscripts Preserved in the University Library, Cambridge* (1876). In 1866 he was appointed Rabbi as Praeceptor in Rabbinic and Talmudic Literature. Following the 1871 Tests Act, he became the first Reader in Talmudic and Rabbinical Literature. These positions helped him play a pivotal role in establishing rabbinic scholarship as an integral part of oriental studies at Cambridge.

Judah Segal

War hero and Jewish
history scholar
1912–2003

Judah Segal was born to
Lithuanian parents in Newcastle-
upon-Tyne. His father Moses
was a Hebrew scholar and
rabbi. Judah followed in those
footsteps and was recognised as
an outstanding student of Semitic languages, winning the Tyrwhitt
scholarship for Hebrew at Cambridge. His studies however, were
interrupted by the Second World War. During the war, Segal used
his knowledge of Arabic to first work with the Sudanese government
and then with MI6 in Cairo. After his introduction to SAS founder
David Stirling, Segal was sent behind enemy lines in north Africa to
report on General Rommel's movements. He hid with local Arabs and
his reports saved thousands of Allied lives. In 1942 he was awarded
the Military Cross. After the war, Segal was appointed to London's
School of Oriental and African Studies, where he lectured in Semitic
languages. In 1961 he was made Head of the Near and Middle
Eastern Department. Segal published many works that increased
understanding of Jewish history, including his *The Hebrew Passover
From Earliest Times to 70AD*. Segal was Vice-President of the Reform
Synagogues of Great Britain and Director of Leo Baeck Jewish
seminary, which he helped to save from closure.

Joseph Shapotshnick

Maverick religious figure
and "miracle-worker"
1882–1937

Shapotshnick was born in Kishinev
(then in the Russian Empire,
now the capital of Moldova)
and was the son of Yehuda Leib
Shapotshnick, a Hasidic leader
known as Belsitzer Rebbe. Following
his father's death in 1896, Shapotshnick and his mother moved to
Odessa, Ukraine, where he studied at the city's university. In 1908 he
published *Kedushas H-Shem*, which explored the cabbalistic meanings
of the name of God. In 1913 he moved to London's East End, where he
would become a controversial figure. Despite publishing a number of
books and pamphlets on religious themes (his best-known publication
Shass ha-gadol she-bi-gedolim was published in 1919), he never obtained
a salaried rabbinical position and was considered a maverick by the
Orthodox religious establishment. He gained a reputation as a "miracle-
worker" and was consulted by both Jews and non-Jews on medical
issues. His forging of documents in support of agunot (women who
were unable to obtain a religious divorce from their husbands, making
future marriages unrecognised under Jewish law), prompted widespread
criticism from religious leaders both in Britain and abroad. Despite his
controversial status, when Shapotshnick died in 1937 thousands of
mourners attended his funeral procession along Whitechapel Road.
His popularity is perhaps explained by his generosity (he gave two-
thirds of his income to charity) and his campaigning for the welfare
and education of immigrant Jews in the East End.

Ernest Julius "Walter" Simon

Recreated the sounds of spoken
Chinese throughout history
1893–1981

Ernest Julius "Walter" Simon
was born in Berlin. He studied
romance and classical philology
at the University of Berlin.
Simon worked at the Higher
Library Service at Berlin University from 1919, studying Chinese
under Otto Franke. He went on exchange to the National Library of
Peking in 1932. He lectured in Chinese at the University of Berlin
from 1926 until 1932 when he became an extraordinary professor
of Chinese. In 1934 he fled to London to escape the Nazis. In
1936 Simon began his academic career in England at the School
of Oriental and African Studies with a lecturing post and became
a reader in Chinese at the University of London two years later. He
was a professor of Chinese from 1947 until 1960 when he retired
and was made Emeritus Professor. Simon then took up a number of
visiting posts at various global universities including Toronto, the
ANU (Australian National University in Canberra) and Tokyo. He was
appointed a CBE in 1961. In his work as a sinologist Simon made
significant contributions to historical Chinese phonology and to the
study of the sino-tibetan languages.

Charles Singer

Helped establish the history
of medicine as a discipline
1876–1960

Charles Singer was born in
London to Charlotte and Simeon
Singer. Simeon was a lecturer at
Jews' College and later rabbi of
the New West End Synagogue.
Young Charles learned Hebrew
and biblical literature from his father. Singer was interested in
the study of both medicine and zoology. He studied the latter at
Magdalen College Oxford and then returned to medicine, graduating
in 1903. Before teaching at Oxford, Singer worked as a doctor in
Singapore, London, Brighton and at the Cancer Hospital. He is
best known as a historian of medicine and in 1912 he became a
founder member of the history of medicine section of the Royal
Society of Medicine, later becoming its president. Along with his
wife Dorothea he dedicated his time to improving the discipline,
investing quantities of his own money into the subject. He wrote the
highly regarded *Studies in the History and Method of Science*. This was
followed by *The Evolution of Anatomy* (1925), which was considered
the first serious study of the subject in English. A later *History of
Technology* illustrated Singer's wide academic interest. During the
Second World War the Singers assisted many refugees from Nazi
Europe and were active in the Society for the Protection of Science
and Learning.

Hans Singer
Attempted to balance the
inequality of world trade
1910–2006

Hans Singer was born in
Elberfeld, Germany. He changed
his plans to become a doctor
after listening to a series of
economics lectures from the
Austrian economist Joseph
Schumpeter at Bonn University. In 1934, Singer fled Nazi Germany
and became one of John Maynard Keynes's first PhD students at
Cambridge. As well as transforming Singer's intellectual horizons,
Keynes obtained his release when he was interned as an enemy
alien. Singer's real work began at the end of the war when he took
on a role as the UN's leading economist, tasked with rebuilding the
devastated European countries and developing the economies of
the third world. He is best known for the Prebisch-Singer thesis
he produced with Raul Prebisch in 1949. They argued that the
reason for declining trade in poorer countries was that exporters
of agricultural commodities were at a disadvantage when compared
with the importers. Singer's ideas were born not of cold theory but
of observation and were often dismissed by mainstream economists.
Singer's efforts to solve world hunger were recognised with the UN's
Food for Life award in 2001.

THE COLLEGE IN FINSBURY SQUARE.

Simeon Singer

Translator of the *Authorised Daily Prayer Book*

1846–1906

Simeon Singer was born in London, the son of a Hungarian father and English mother. His academic aptitude was noticed from an early age and, following a brief period of schooling in Austria, he received a Barnett Myers Scholarship at the age of 13. He attended the day school of Jews' College in Finsbury Square, known for its strong language curriculum, and became fluent in French, German and biblical Hebrew. He stayed at the College to receive rabbinical training under its principal Michael Friedländer, becoming a minister and eventually headmaster of the day school, where he remained for 12 years. He combined this with ministries at Borough Synagogue, Walworth (from 1867) and the New West End Synagogue (from 1878 until his death). Singer was particularly known for his talents as a preacher, and despite his traditional background was open to reform within the community. Some of his innovations included introducing Bible readings in English, conducting sermons for children and supporting the admission of women as choristers. The author of a number of published works, Singer's most enduring is his English translation of the *Authorised Daily Prayer Book*. Originally published in 1890, it remains the standard prayer book of the majority of the UK's Orthodox Jews, and is known affectionately as "Singer's Siddur".

Piero Sraffa

Founded the neo-Ricardian
school of economics
1898–1983

Piero Sraffa was born in Turin,
Italy. His parents were affluent
Jews. Sraffa graduated from
the University of Turin in 1920
with a doctorate in law. He
joined the University of Perugia
in 1924 as Associate Professor of Political Economy before taking
up a professorship at the University of Cagliari in 1926. Sraffa was
forced to leave Italy after falling foul of Mussolini and, with the
assistance of economist John Maynard Keynes, became a lecturer
at the Cambridge faculty of economics. He took up a fellowship
at Trinity College, Cambridge in 1939. Sraffa mixed with great
thinkers such as Ludwig Wittgenstein and Antonio Gramsci, and his
own contribution to the intellectual debates of the 20th century
was considerable. He brought new insight to Ricardo's surplus
theory and clarified the theory of value system in *Production of
Commodities by Means of Commodities* (1960), a work that founded
the neo-Ricardian school of economics. Sraffa began working on
his ambitious edition of Ricardo's correspondence in 1930 and
developed a consistent argument over the course of 11 volumes
(1951–73). In 1961 he was awarded the Stockholm Academy of
Science Gold Medal.

Aurel Stein

Archaeologist of the
treasures of Asia
1862–1943

Aurel Stein was born in Hungary
to merchant Nathan Stein and
his wife Anna. The family was
comfortably off and advocated
assimilation. Stein was baptised
into the Lutheran church. He
studied Sanskrit, Old Persian and philology at the Universities of
Vienna, Leipzig and Tubingen. In 1887 he made his first trip to India.
He enjoyed a number of positions at different Indian universities
and also made an expedition to the Peshawar Valley. Although Stein
chose to settle in England, he is best known as a discoverer of
ancient communities. During three expeditions in the early 1900s,
Stein travelled to Chinese Turkestan where, along the Silk Road, he
uncovered the remains of a previously unknown civilisation. The items
Stein discovered included coins, textiles, documents and manuscripts;
many of these are now housed in the British Library, the British
Museum and the V&A. At a site in Tunhuang, Stein reached the Cave
of the Thousand Buddhas, where he found more manuscripts and a
copy of the *Diamond Sutra* from 868 CE, the earliest known printed
book. Stein did not return to Judaism but used his modest savings
to help members of his family fleeing persecution during the Second
World War.

Edward Ullendorff

Historian and scholar of
Semitic languages
1920–2011

Ullendorff was born in Zürich and
attended the Gymnasium Graues
Kloster in Berlin. In 1938 he fled
Nazi Germany for Palestine (then
under the British Mandate) and
studied Semitic languages at the
Hebrew University of Jerusalem. During the Second World War he
joined the British Army and in 1941, due to his knowledge of Ethiopian
Semitic languages, was posted to Eritrea, newly liberated from Italian
rule. There he established the first newspaper in the Tigrinya language
and as editor recruited Woldeab Woldemariam, later known as the
father of Eritrea. In Ethiopia Ullendorff met Emperor Haile Selassie I,
whose memoir he would later translate. Following the war Ullendorff
returned to Palestine but in 1948, with relations between Jewish
and Arab communities deteriorating, he left to complete a DPhil in
Ethiopian languages at the Oxford Institute of Colonial Studies. In the
distinguished academic career that followed, Ullendorff held positions
at the universities of St Andrews (1950–59) and Manchester (1959–
64) and the School of Oriental and African Studies (1964–82), where
he remained Professor Emeritus until his death. In 2012 the British
Academy established the Edward Ullendorf Medal, awarded annually
for scholarly distinction and achievements in the field of Semitic
languages and Ethiopian studies. Ullendorff's books include *The
Ethiopians: An Introduction to Country and People* (1966), *Ethiopia and
the Bible* (1968) and the memoir *The Two Zions* (1988).

Geza Vermes

He revealed the Dead Sea
Scrolls to the world
1924–2013

Geza Vermes was born in
Hungary to parents Terezia and
Erno. His family converted to
Catholicism when Geza began
school. Later, Geza studied to
become a Catholic priest, an
undertaking that saved his life, as during the Holocaust he was hidden
by the Church. Sadly, his parents died in an unknown location. Vermes
attended the Catholic University of Louvain. Here, six years after the
discovery of the Dead Sea Scrolls, Vermes completed the first ever
doctorate on the documents, entitled *Manuscripts from the Judean
Desert*, in which he asserted that the sect that authored the works
originated in the second century BCE. In 1962 Vermes published an
English translation of the scrolls that has not been out of print since.
Throughout his career Vermes argued with Israeli archaeologists
who housed the scrolls to obtain wider access. In 1965 Vermes was
appointed the first Reader of Jewish Studies at Oxford. He published
many works on early Christianity and the "Historical Jesus" and was
congratulated by the US House of Representatives for "inspiring and
educating the world." Vermes left the Catholic Church when he met
his future wife, the poet Pamela Hobson Curle (a married woman). He
reasserted his Jewish identity from 1957, and later joined the Liberal
Jewish Synagogue.

By accident or grace, for over more than half a century I have had the good fortune to be actively involved in the saga of the Dead Sea Scrolls."

Geza Vermes

Arthur Waley

An ambassador for the
East and the West
1889–1966

Arthur Waley was born in
Tunbridge Wells, Kent. His
father, David Schloss, was one
of the first Jews to be elected
to a college scholarship.
Arthur changed his name from
Schloss to Waley in 1914 to avoid anti-German prejudice in Britain.
Waley was raised in Wimbledon and educated at Rugby School. He
excelled academically and won an open scholarship to study classics
at King's College, Cambridge. Waley's greatest achievement was
introducing ideas from the east to a western audience. In 1913 he
found his calling in the oriental prints department at the British
Museum, where, tasked with making an index of the Chinese and
Japanese painters in the museum, he began to teach himself both
languages. In 1916 he privately printed 52 translations of Chinese
poems and, in 1919, Stanley Unwin published Waley's first volume *A
Hundred and Seventy Chinese Poems*. He was neither an expert in
the languages nor the best poet but his combination of both was
unrivalled. His most ambitious project, *Genji Monogatari* by Murasaki
Shikibu, took him almost ten years to translate. Waley was appointed
CBE and Companion of Honour, and also received the Queen's Gold
Medal for Poetry. Interestingly, he never actually visited East Asia.

Bernard Waley-Cohen

Mayor who built bridges
between faiths
1914–1991

Bernard Nathaniel Waley-
Cohen was born in London.
He was the first son of pioneer
of industry Robert Waley-
Cohen and his wife Alice
Violet Beddington. Bernard
was educated at Clifton College, Bristol, where he boarded at
Polack's, the Jewish house founded by his grandfather Lionel Cohen.
Bernard went up to Magdalene College, Oxford, to read history
and left in 1936 to embark upon a career in business. Waley-Cohen
was unable to serve in the Second World War due to his defective
eyesight, so turned instead to public service. He was attached first to
the Port of London Emergency Service, and then to the Ministry of
Fuel and Power alongside Harold Wilson. After the war the markets
reopened and Waley-Cohen found success as a banker, serving as the
Vice-Chairman of the Union Bank of Israel. He became Alderman and
Lieutenant of the City of London and was knighted in 1957. In 1960
he became only the seventh Jew to be elected Lord Mayor of London,
and in 1961 was elevated to a baronetcy. A proud Jew, he was a
passionate advocate of interfaith relations and during his mayoralty
reached out to Muslim and Christian faith leaders. He was buried in
Willesden Jewish cemetery. Waley-Cohen demonstrated his respect
for his mayoral position by taking his chain of office and his ermine
robes with him whenever he travelled.

ARISTOTELIS
ETHICA EVDEMIA

R. R. WALZER ET J. M. MINGAY

Richard Walzer
A Jewish scholar of Islam
1900–1975

Richard Walzer was born in Berlin to businessman Max and his wife Elfriede. After completing his high school education Walzer began to study medicine and Hebrew. However, he soon discovered that his interest lay in ancient Greek and classics. He began to break new ground in the field early on, with his doctoral thesis. Walzer claimed that the *Magna Moralia*, thought to be Aristotle's oldest work on ethics, was actually the product of the school of Theophrastus. Many agreed and subsequent studies of the work all followed this line. Walzer's main contribution was in the study of Greek thought in Arabic intellectual communities. He offered new interpretations of ancient Greek fragments that had been spread among the Islamic world and he offered commentary on the various changes that these fragments had undergone as a result of their environment. In the late 1930s, while on holiday in Rome, Walzer realised the threat posed by Nazism and did not return home to Germany, instead teaching in Italy before making his home in Oxford.

Stephen Winsten
Biographer
1893–1991

Born Samuel Weinstein, Winsten was from a Russian-Jewish background and grew up in Hackney, north London. As a young man he was part of a group of Jewish artists and intellectuals (also including Isaac Rosenberg) who were subsequently known as the "Whitechapel Boys". During the First World War Winsten's claim to be a conscientious objector was rejected and he was imprisoned for two years. He was eventually released in 1919 and was able to resume his work as a writer, becoming the arts editor of the literary journal *Voices*. He became known for his work on George Bernard Shaw, his neighbour in the Hertfordshire village of Ayot St Lawrence. He would ultimately write four books on him, including *Days With Bernard Shaw*, an account of the time he spent with Shaw prior to the playwright's death in 1950. His other published work includes a biography of the writer and animal rights campaigner Henry Salt. Following his marriage to the sculptor Clara Birnberg, they both changed their surnames to Winsten and became Quaker humanists. Their daughter Ruth Harrison (1920–2000) was a leading campaigner for animal rights and their son Christopher (1923–2005) was a professor of mathematics at the University of Essex.

Ludwig Wittgenstein

Possibly the greatest philosopher
of the twentieth century
1899–1951

Ludwig Wittgenstein was born
in Vienna, Austria, to one of
Europe's richest families. His
paternal great-grandfather and
maternal grandfather were Jewish.
For a time he attended the same
school as Adolf Hitler, who was six days older than he. Wittgenstein
inherited his father's fortune in 1913, then, in a period of intense de-
pression following the First World War, gave it all away to his siblings.
He studied mechanical engineering in Berlin and then at the Victoria
University of Manchester. From 1929 to 1947 he taught at the University of Cambridge, where he came to be regarded by many as the
greatest philosopher since Immanuel Kant. His life is usually separated out into two periods: the early and the late Wittgenstein. This
division maps onto his two great works: *Tractatus* and *Philosophical
Investigations*. Upon completing the first, Wittgenstein declared that
he had solved all of philosophy's problems and began to pursue other livelihoods as a gardener and teacher. Upon reflection he realised
he had not yet said all he wanted to and embarked on his second
significant work. Although baptised a Catholic and professing atheism
at different times during his life, Wittgenstein referred to himself as a
Jew, saying, "My thoughts are 100 % Hebraic". When he learned the
fate of European Jews in the death camps, Wittgenstein exemplified
his own theory of the inadequacy of language by refusing to speak;
instead, he silently wept.

Joseph Wolff

A missionary with a
taste for danger
1795–1862

Joseph Wolff was born in
Germany to Orthodox
rabbi David Levi and his wife
Sarah. Wolff was sent to a
Protestant school as his father
hoped he would qualify as
a doctor. Joseph, however, rejected his parents' religion and was
baptised as a Roman Catholic in 1812. Travelling to Rome, Wolff was
outspokenly critical of Roman Catholic doctrine and consequently
was exiled to England. Able to speak 14 languages, Wolff in 1821
embarked upon his missionary, which took him all over the world. His
travels were full of excitement; in Kabul he was robbed and forced
to walk 600 miles in the nude. Later, he travelled to Uzbekistan
to ascertain the fate of two English intelligence officers. He was
threatened with execution but his knowledge of the language
endeared him to the locals, who helped him escape. He published a
book about his experiences, *Narrative of a Mission to Bokhara*, which
reached seven editions. Wolff travelled to America, where he
preached to Congress and where, in 1837, he was ordained as a
Church of England deacon.

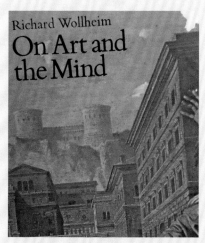

Richard Wollheim
On Art and the Mind

Richard Wollheim

Taught us a different
way of seeing
1923–2003

Richard Wollheim was born in
London to Eric Wollheim, an
agent for Sergei Diaghilev's
ballets, and his wife Constance.
Richard became known as the
philosopher who successfully
fused psychoanalysis with the philosophy of art. *Wollheim's Art and
its Objects* posited the idea that the true understanding of a painting
results from the artist's organisation of the surface on which rests
the paint. This idea, developed in his later book *Painting as an Art*,
came to be referred to as "seeing in". Wollheim argued that, in viewing
art in this way, one can begin to deduce the artist's "real" intention
and that this in turn created a shared culture between artist and
viewer; in a painting of a dog, for example, it is possible to see not
just the figure of an animal but also the artist's intention in the
dog's eyes: loyalty, love or happiness. Although born into a Jewish
family, Wollheim was raised Christian and later turned away from faith
altogether. He liked to champion the underdog, whether it be the
black Civil Rights movement or the plight of the Palestinians.

Photography credits

p. 3 under the Creative Commons (CC) licence © National Museum in Krakow, p. 6 © Jewish Museum London / Les Editions Albert René – Goscinny / Uderzo, pp. 9, 12, 21, 24, 28, 36, 49, 53, 57, 59, 60, 63 ,71, 72, 80, 89, 95, 99, 101, 110, 113, 179, 185, 191, 192, 193, 194, 211, 226, 232, 237, 252 under the Creative Commons (CC) licence, pp. 11, 37, 38, 39, 40, 41, 42, 43, 45, 46, 48, 55, 56, 66, 67, 69, 70, 74, 76, 94, 100, 108, 109, 126, 137, 138, 146, 156, 158, 160, 170, 187, 188, 197, 198, 203, 206, 209, 214, 218, 220, 224, 238, 240, 245, 246, 257, 261, 267, 275, 276, 277, 279 from the Public Domain, p. 21 © Library of Congress, Geography and Map Division, p. 33 © Arcaid Images / Alamy Stock Photo, 44, 47, 50, 54, 88, 107, 139, 149, 152, 157, 190, 213, 264, 273, 274 © National Portrait Gallery, London, p. 51 © Jewish Historical Society, p.52 © CATO, p. 58 © Isaiah Berlin, pp. 61, 64, 92, 93, 129, 184, 205 © Rex Features, p. 62 © Gary Italiander, pp. 65, 114, 120, 167, 204 © Jewish Museum, London, p. 68 © Patrick Nairne / Alamy Stock Photo, p. 96 © Norbert Elias Foundation, pp. 102, 103, 104, 210, 221, 223, 225, 250, 254 © Top Foto, p. 105 © Berkley College, p. 111 © Creative Commons/Ferdinand Schmutzer, p. 112 © Chronicle / Alamy Stock Photo, pp. 31, 134, 200, 260 © LSE Archive, p. 132 by anne Geras © courtesty of Adele Geras, p. 133 © martingilbert.com, p. 136 © Anthropology. com, pp. 141, 217, 228, 233 © Webb & Webb, p. 148 © Getty Images, p. 144 under the Creative Commons (CC) licence © NASA, p. 148 photograph by Sharon Chazan © Naomi Gryn, p. 150 © Kurt Hahn Foundation, p. 162 © Birkbeck College, p. 164 © Gerry Cambridge, p. 165 Courtesy Rob Ward, p. 168 © Art Kowalsky / Alamy Stock Photo, p. 174 World Image Archive / Alamy Stock Photo, p. 188 © OCHJS, p. 189 © Peter Loft, p. 196 under the Creative Commons (CC) licence © Wellcome Trust, p. 199 © Geni, p. 208 © Iranica Online, p. 212 © National Library of Israel, p. 244 © University of Glasgow, p. 251 © The Masters and Fellows of Peterhouse Cambridge, p. 255 © Courtesy of Rodker Family, p. 256 © UCL, p. 258 © Raphael Samuel History Centre, p. 266 © UN Archive, p. 269 © Wellcome Library, p. 270 © SOAS Library, p. 271 © World Service PR Image

The publisher has made every effort to contact the current copyright holders and obtain permission to reproduce the images included in this book. Any omissions are entirely unintentional, and further details should be addressed to the Jewish Museum London to be included in any reprint.